About Island Press

Since 1984, the nonprofit organization Island Press has been stimulating, shaping, and communicating ideas that are essential for solving environmental problems worldwide. With more than 1,000 titles in print and some 30 new releases each year, we are the nation's leading publisher on environmental issues. We identify innovative thinkers and emerging trends in the environmental field. We work with world-renowned experts and authors to develop cross-disciplinary solutions to environmental challenges.

Island Press designs and executes educational campaigns, in conjunction with our authors, to communicate their critical messages in print, in person, and online using the latest technologies, innovative programs, and the media. Our goal is to reach targeted audiences—scientists, policy makers, environmental advocates, urban planners, the media, and concerned citizens—with information that can be used to create the framework for long-term ecological health and human well-being.

Island Press gratefully acknowledges major support from The Bobolink Foundation, Caldera Foundation, The Curtis and Edith Munson Foundation, The Forrest C. and Frances H. Lattner Foundation, The JPB Foundation, The Kresge Foundation, The Summit Charitable Foundation, Inc., and many other generous organizations and individuals.

The opinions expressed in this book are those of the author(s) and do not necessarily reflect the views of our supporters.

Inclusive Transportation

Inclusive Transportation

A MANIFESTO FOR REPAIRING
DIVIDED COMMUNITIES

Veronica O. Davis

 **ISLAND**PRESS | Washington | Covelo

Library of Congress Control Number: 2022948620

All Island Press books are printed on environmentally responsible materials.

Manufactured in the United States of America
10 9 8 7 6 5

Keywords: Black Women Bike, community input, congestion, connectivity, curriculum, diversity, empathy, equity, health outcomes, last-mile connections, leadership, mobility, neighborhood disinvestment, public engagement, road congestion, technology, traffic engineering, transportation infrastructure, transportation planning, vision

To Eliana, Owen, and Olivia.
You are the next generation.
May you continue the legacy.

Contents

Foreword

By tamika l. butler, esq.

FOR DECADES, BLACK PLANNERS, public health professionals, engineers, and the community stakeholders who we represent have been calling for racial equity in all facets of urban planning, allied fields, and Black life. Prior to 2020, our words and thoughts were greeted with applause, praise, and maybe a mention via social media or an academic citation. In 2020, the uneven impacts of the COVID-19 pandemic, the daily stories of racism in shared urban spaces such as bike lanes, parks, and sidewalks, and our common witness of George Floyd's murder in a public street placed "racial equity" center stage for urban planning professionals. As the world protested the multiple unjust murders of Black people, the nation's power structure offered appeasements. But was real change on the way? Was real action a possibility?

As Veronica O. Davis wrote this book throughout 2022, the pandemic continued, and still continues, to disproportionately impact Indigenous, Black, and Brown people. Add other identities and those disparities increase: people living with disabilities, people living in poverty, femme-identified and genderqueer people; the list could go on. The power structures that at first were willing to adapt in order to respond to a deadly, highly transmissible virus have begun to reassert their prime directives—productivity and profit building.

National planning organizations and conferences have returned to organizing events that cater to their predominantly White, male, able-bodied, heterosexual, and privileged leadership and membership. Organizations that continue to tout equity, diversity, and inclusion are still hiring and voting in all-White leadership structures that fail to represent the diverse tapestry that is the backbone of the United States.

This book joins the chorus of the many Black professionals who have been asking their peers to engage in new ways of thinking, listening, and governing. Most important, it does so by offering concrete advice that planners and allied professionals can take to assess their own privilege, interrogate power, and actively shift those dynamics in their work. For many of us, 2020 was just another year of injustice. We know that the anti-racist future we believe in has not arrived. This lack of progress is due, in part, to the lack of action taken by those in positions of power. Too often, those in power with an ability to bring about change cite an inability to know where to begin. I hope those leaders, as well as scholars, students, and anyone interested in justice, read this manifesto for repairing divided communities. More than one hundred years after the Tulsa massacre (one of many acts of White annihilation of thriving Black spaces in cities), three years after George Floyd's murder, and moments away from the next Black death, Veronica provides a practical, thoughtful, and empathetic step-by-step guide to anyone who cares about people, wants to build just communities, and hopes to serve the world. This book will, can, and should serve as a handbook or manual for people to refer to at every step of a process. With the humor, grace, and realness I have come to love and cherish in my friend, Veronica guides people through how to do transportation planning right.

Veronica is a determined, dynamic, daring doer and dreamer. I am also lucky to call her a dear friend, a coconspirator, a colleague, and a sister. In the years I have learned and grown with Veronica, she has always been a leading voice in what inclusive transportation can do as we seek to repair and redress the harms done to our divided communities. Like all Black women practicing, teaching, and learning in different aspects of the planning and urban placemaking worlds, we have shared many conversations about the ways we experience and process shared fears for our families and our futures that were felt long before 2020, when many dared to finally confront the racial inequities built into this country's systems, institutions, and built environment.

I feel changed by reading Veronica's book. I hope you feel the same. Turn the page, get started on, or continue, your justice journey, and when you finish, make a commitment to do more than just talk about equity. The just future Veronica's child and my children deserve is within reach. Like many leaders, Veronica will play a role in getting us there. You can play a role, too, or you can get out of the way.

Preface

WHAT DO WE OWE EACH OTHER? Do we all have duties to society, or do we get to live and let live? Adhere to social contracts, or balance the needs of the greater good with our own?

To be completely honest, if you are paying attention to the tenor of the discussions around transportation in the United States, it might seem that people who live here are selfish and in a hurry. Perhaps not in all regards, but when it comes to getting from point A to point B, most of us come across as unwilling to endure any minor inconvenience for the country's greater good. There is an unwillingness to abide by rules of the road, which breaks the social contract.

People with careers in transportation see this selfishness and hurriedness play out every single day. Traffic engineers install stoplights and people run them intentionally because heaven forbid they should be inconvenienced by having to sit at a red light for ninety seconds. People illegally block crosswalks with their parked cars because they will "just be a minute" while they run into a building to grab something "quickly." Instead of pulling over on the side of the road or waiting until the next time they stop, drivers attempt to text while driving.

People drive over the speed limit because they need to get to their destination as quickly as possible. These me-first behaviors are often the precursors to crashes that lead to serious injuries and death. How do you plan and design safer roads when you know these attitudes and behaviors exist?

I am not anti-car, nor am I part of some secret lobby out to rid the world of cars or, as some journalists opine, a soldier in the war against cars. However, I do not think it is sustainable to live in an urban or suburban community where driving a car is your only option. And yet I see many people unwilling to acknowledge that car-centric transportation makes other options more dangerous and difficult to implement.

When I was in middle school, we played in the middle of the street. If a car came down the street, someone would yell "Car!" and we would scatter to the side of the road to let the car by. The driver would slow to a crawl just in case a wiggly kid darted into the street. This highlighted a mutual understanding and respect that we were sharing the same space. Fast-forward a handful of decades and children are struck and killed by drivers as they walk to school with friends, ride their bicycles, and even stand waiting at a bus stop.

We should all be willing to do whatever it takes to make our transportation system safe for children. One would think. But in my experience, I have seen the opposite. I have had many projects where people were not willing to deal with any inconvenience to make roads safer. Show them data that they will be delayed only one minute? Nope. They do not want to be delayed. Try to take away on-street parking? Hell hath no fury like a community that may lose parking.

As I think about how we can repair divided communities, I know it will require empathy, compassion, and willingness to accept minor inconveniences for the greater good. And people may even find they can still drive their cars, but life is better when people have options, adults with disabilities and children can move around safely, and older adults can still visit their friends when driving becomes more difficult.

To Be Completely Honest . . .

There is a part of me that worries whether the transportation industry has the ability to change or even wants to change. The title of the book is about repairing divided communities. How do you change a system that was never designed to be equitable? How do you change the system that divided the communities in the first place? What happens if you try to move it in the opposite direction? What if it is like a pendulum, which moves in the opposite direction, one I would consider progress, but then swings back to where it was—or perhaps farther, resulting in more communities destroyed and lives lost?

There are pioneers who are the leaders in designing multi-passenger transportation and bicycle infrastructure. There are believers who look to examples of other countries that have made the commitment and investment to create cities that are walkable and bikeable. But there are still plenty among us who are perfectly fine with destroying a community to widen a highway or a roadway to "relieve congestion," who believe that the ends justify the means. They are willing to sacrifice communities, mostly Black, Brown, low income, or all three, for what they see as the greater good or for moving other people and goods through the community.

That last group still holds power in many state departments of transportation, consultant companies, contracting companies, state capitols, and even Capitol Hill. Consultants and contractors see the dollar signs. Elected officials' campaigns are funded by people with deep pockets, and the officials are in power to ensure companies continue to make money. To be fair to some state departments of transportation, they are beholden to the laws, regulations, and performance metrics created by their state legislature or executive branch, depending on the state, which funnels massive amounts of funding toward car-centric projects. It is a complicated and long-term process to change that structure—it will take patience, even as people are killed needlessly and communities are razed. But the more people there are who understand what must change, and who work together to envision a transportation system that actually provides freedom for all and is safe and affordable, the more likely we will be to achieve it. I hope the ideas in the pages ahead will give you insight and support for the challenges you'll face in your work to shift how people living in the United States think about transportation and for the planning, design, and implementation of the projects themselves.

To Be Completely Honest . . .

This book was harder to write than I expected. Between the time I started my outline and when I completed the final draft, I had a baby, sold the company I cofounded, and became an executive in a very large local government agency. Oh, and there was a global pandemic that upended our lives.

As my life changed in profound and unexpected ways—along with our entire world—I found myself struggling to find the right words to articulate my point. Some of the struggle was in finding the balance between nuance and making the book understandable to different readers. The other part was in understanding when I was dancing around an issue to avoid saying what needed to be said.

I am still learning that self-doubt is a lie that will always trap you where you are. It will make you feel small. Throughout this writing process, I had moments of self-doubt about being "the expert." What makes someone an expert? Is there a magical ceremony where one officially becomes an expert? Does writing a book solidify one's expertise?

Does someone need a doctorate? Do men ask themselves this question? I remember a conversation with colleagues whom I call my heart and soul trust where we questioned who gets to decide who's the authority on a topic.

Being Black and a woman in a White- and man-dominated industry is enough to create doubt. My parents gave me the lecture most Black parents give their children: "You have to be twice as good to even be seen as an equal." It is a lecture that propelled me to work hard in college and earn a double master's degree from an Ivy League school. Because if I have two master's, then no one can say they were given to me, because what school would give away two master's? I even briefly started a doctoral program so that no one could say I did not deserve it. However, that lecture still sometimes makes me question whether what I am doing is good enough. Is my book twice as good—good enough to be seen as equal?

There were times when I wanted to call my editor and tell her I gave it my best shot and maybe this was not meant to be. We each have a choice, to listen to the voice that says we cannot do it or to ignore the voice and do it anyway.

And so, I continued typing. I continued because there is a younger generation who want a better future for themselves and the generations after them. I believe my professional and personal experiences provide another point of view and vision for the future of the industry. I continued to write because there are communities that have been harmed and continue to be harmed.

To Be Completely Honest . . .

As of the initial publishing of this book, I am the director of transportation and drainage operations for the City of Houston. I started this book well before submitting my résumé for the position, and the book's focus is on my life and professional experiences prior to being in Houston. However, as I continued to complete drafts, I had internal conflicts between Veronica the consultant/advocate/community journalist, who wants transportation leaders to be bold and to make hard decisions, and Veronica the decision-maker, who is balancing all the needs and demands of a city with a finite number of resources. And who, even more, frankly, wants to keep her job. I went from an observer to a decision-maker. Whether in Houston or wherever my career takes me next, I kept envisioning an irate citizen holding up my book with highlighted quotes. But that is ultimately the point, correct? To be better and to be accountable to the public, particularly in communities that have repeatedly been negatively impacted by the transportation system. There are learning opportunities for us all, and we must be willing to show up and have an honest conversation. I hope this book will be a starting point for many of those.

Introduction

SHOW ME A TRANSPORTATION NETWORK and I will tell you the values of the decision-makers who designed it. In places I have visited, such as Antigua, Guatemala, and Brussels, Belgium, I have seen how very different parts of the world can have in common transportation networks that focus on people and on places to walk. Both of these cities have pedestrian-only streets, which allow for a vibrant atmosphere and the ability to people-watch from an outdoor patio while sipping coffee. Where I grew up, in Maplewood, New Jersey, a small suburban community outside of New York City, I was able to walk to school and playgrounds without adult supervision. During the one summer I had Rollerblades, I was able to coast down the hill in the street without fear of being struck by someone driving.

Even though these communities reflect different eras and cultures, they are all walkable places with human-scale design. All three of these communities were built before the invention of the automobile. Maplewood was originally constructed for people walking or using horses. Antigua, Guatemala, has many of the original cobblestone streets, which make for an uncomfortable drive.

As an adult living in Washington, DC, I lived for eight of the fifteen years without a car, dependent on public transportation, walking, and biking. I lived in three areas of the city within walking distance of a Metrorail station, which made getting to work and meeting up with friends relatively seamless. However, I did live in a part of the city that made me dependent on the bus system, which was designed to get people downtown during the workday but made it impossible to get to church or even a grocery store on the weekend within my community.

My travels have also taken me around the United States to communities designed around the automobile and communities destroyed by the automobile. Many cities and suburbs bleed together in my memory because they all have similar layouts. They have eight- to ten-lane roadways lined with strip malls and are hostile to anyone not traveling in a vehicle. Often, children are driven to school in large sport utility vehicles because it is not safe for them to walk or bike to school.

People in the transportation industry play an important role in shaping communities and future generations. If you are an engineer, planner, community advocate, elected leader, or journalist, you are part of the transportation ecosystem (some may even call it an echo chamber), making decisions and crafting narratives today that will impact where and how people will move in the future. The Centers for Disease Control and Prevention developed a framework of factors that lead to positive health outcomes. Whether your community is walkable or is hostile to people who are not in a vehicle is a factor of the social determinants of health for people living in that community.[1] A car-centric community is not a factor that leads to positive health outcomes.

Unfortunately, we inherited a transportation network that reflects decades of decision-making by our predecessors who ceded communities to motor vehicles. Communities where people could once walk, bike, and use public transit were divided, leveled, and reshaped to make way for the interstate highways and wide streets designed by our pre-decessors. Ideally, the transportation network would connect people to jobs, education, food, opportunities, and each other. But this has not actually been the case for decades. There is a lot to redo, and in some cases dismantle, and transportation projects can be expensive and take many years to implement.

We have a choice of whether to continue to use the old tools of our predecessors or to shift the paradigm to right historical injustices by designing a network that is inclusive of all people while also preparing for the future. We have an opportunity to shape our future.

As the old saying goes, you cannot solve a problem with the same thinking that created it. This book aims to discuss the inequities related to our existing transportation network and how new projects are planned and built and to examine what we can do to create a more equitable network. If you have heard people using the term "equity" and want to know more, this is a book for you.

Even if your work does not directly involve transportation planning or implementation, I hope you take away from this book tools that will help you be more vocal about transportation projects that affect your community. Perhaps you will be inspired to attend a community meeting, complete a survey, write to an elected official, or author an opinion editorial for your local newspaper. If you are unable to move safely around your community without being in a motor vehicle, maybe you will advocate for safety improvements. If you are frustrated because lanes for vehicles are being reallocated to other uses, such as transit-only lanes and bike lanes, I hope you will gain some empathy for the people who rely on these modes for safe travel.

If you understand the inequities and do not know what to do about them, I aim to help you navigate, reflect, and develop action steps. Every plan, design, and written policy gives you the ability to change an entire community with the stroke of a keyboard key or click of the mouse.

Even when you make data-driven decisions, the data still reflect values and goals directed by the project's values and goals.

As you read the chapters, you may have a specific project in mind where you want to do an inclusive community and stakeholder engagement process that truly guides the technical process. Or you may have had a project go awry, and you want to do a postmortem analysis to evaluate what went wrong and help you develop a clearer sense of what to do differently if you do it again.

Perhaps, at the root, you believe there is a better way to plan, design, construct, operate, and maintain the transportation system. With new technologies and best practices in the world, you know we can plan and design a better transportation system for the future. You have this knowledge, but you do not know what to do with it.

Whether you are a transportation professional or a journalist, you cannot forget the power of narratives and storytelling. Words have meaning. Beyond the plans, policies, and data, the story that is crafted—by politicians, community members, project consultants, and so forth—influences the public. Although it may take more time than the standard approach, it is critically important to communicate and explain the process so that all members of the community can access the information. There is also a need to interrogate community concerns and discern which ones can be addressed and which ones are red herrings, raised to protect or amplify the interests of a small subset but not the community as a whole. This is a skill, and it is largely still not taught to people preparing to be professional engineers or planners. We need to change that—it is fundamental to creating better, more inclusive transportation networks and repairing divided communities.

Today's discussions of equity prompt a lot of different reactions. Thank you for wanting to learn more—though I acknowledge you may be here begrudgingly, skeptically, or with genuine interest. In chapter 2, I provide definitions and frameworks for equity. This chapter will give you a base understanding. Throughout the following chapters, there will be opportunities and questions for reflection to help you unpack the term and how it shows up in your work.

I hope this book feels like a conversation, and I have tried to layer in the understanding of multiple viewpoints from my experiences in the transportation industry and the different communities I have visited or been a consultant in.

Technology Will Not Save Us

Transportation technology is changing faster now than it has for previous generations. Many of the technologies from previous generations centered on the transportation mode itself, such as the automobile, which has evolved into a machine that can go over one hundred miles per hour and be powered by electricity. Recent technologies have assisted with eliminating ownership or shifting the trip to someone else. From a smartphone that fits in the palm of our hand, we can order a ride or even have food, medicine, or alcohol delivered to our doorstep. We can unlock a scooter or unlock a shared vehicle. Even the humble bicycle has transformed into a shared public asset that one can access via the scan of a code. Car companies are racing to deliver vehicles that can operate without a driver.

Technology companies are leading the way into the future with some innovative ideas, such as autonomous shuttles that move around college campuses and even autonomous food delivery to provide access to groceries in communities that do not have a grocery store. However, two major flaws will hold them back from creating equitable transportation networks. One, the companies often lack diversity,[2] which leads to a high-tech version of the inequitable transportation system we have today. This may not be intuitive for people. People may believe technology is the great equalizer for race and gender. However, technology is more a reflection of its designers' thoughts and lived experiences. When technology is mostly designed by men, the needs of women and children may not be considered.

As an example, when technology is designed by people with lighter skin, the design tends to default to lighter skin tones. The technology fails to detect darker skin. A study from the Georgia Institute of Technology points out how the object detection used in autonomous technology has difficulty recognizing darker skin.[3] This can lead to the possibility of self-driving cars being more likely to hit a Black pedestrian. When technology is designed by a person with no disabilities, the final product often has to be customized to work for people with disabilities. For example, an autonomous vehicle company will say that driverless vehicles will help people with disabilities move around. But terms such as "last-mile connection" leave out people with disabilities when the last one hundred feet can still be challenging.

Second, tech companies lack an understanding of transportation. They are applauded and welcomed for disrupting the transportation industry. They will say they can do it faster than government. When there are no rules, it is easy to disrupt. However, once the dust of the disruption settles, communities are left questioning whether they want the technology or whether it has improved equity.[4] Frequently, it has not. For example, the introduction of shared dockless bicycles and scooters may have improved economics for some cities.[5] However, they created issues for people with disabilities, such as when users leave them in the middle of the sidewalk or a curb ramp, creating a tripping hazard or making a sidewalk impassable for someone in a wheelchair. The results have caused cities to create regulations or in some cases ban them altogether.[6]

Technology companies do not always care about unintended consequences. They care about their product, their investors, and their next fundraising series. The pressure to deliver can trump doing what is best for society. So, while tech companies may tout their credentials for thinking creatively and differently, transportation networks are a public good that should serve all equally—and we should be wary of for-profit companies being the knight in shining armor for transportation reform.

Regardless of changes in technology, we cannot lose sight of the fact that people still need to move safely, reliably, and—most important for equity—affordably. As communities continue to grow in population, congestion will get worse if the baseline assumption is that new residents will drive themselves in their own vehicle for every trip. Even with the promise that autonomous vehicles and connected vehicles (vehicles that can communicate with other vehicles and infrastructure) will improve traffic flow, it is still congestion, albeit moving more efficiently, if each person is driving a vehicle alone.

Baseline Assumptions

To keep this book under ten thousand pages, I have assumed that you have a baseline understanding of the impact of redlining, White flight, and capitalism on the building of the interstate highway system and how engineers, planners, and policy makers of previous generations designed the transportation system that we have today. You know that states and cities often constructed highways through neighborhoods where Black, Brown, and low-income people live. You know that communities were constructed with railroads creating separate sides of towns, reflected in the euphemism "the wrong side of the tracks." You are aware that these past decisions have led to an inequitable transportation system.

With those as baseline assumptions, I will not go into a history lesson on the policies and actions that created the inequities. Yet even if this is not your understanding, you are welcome on the journey. Throughout the chapters, I cite resources that take a deeper dive into history that is well documented by historians and researchers. However, I encourage you to take the time to research further.

I will also assume you have been exposed to the term "privilege." Perhaps its most popular use is in the term "White privilege." If the term makes you uncomfortable, I invite you to sit with that discomfort and continue reading. In chapter 4, I explore the concept of power and the privileges that it brings. Depending on identity and background, readers will have different levels of power and privilege in society. Whether reading this for college credit, continuing professional education, or general curiosity, all readers of this book have some form of privilege even to be able to hold this book. The power available to you will differ depending on your profession, where you are in your career, who you know, who knows you, and your proximity to decision-makers.

The Time Is Now

The transportation industry is facing paralysis by analysis. In some cases, it is an analysis of the wrong type of data. We have reports, data, and dissertations that document the inequities in the transportation system. We have all sorts of tools and apps to analyze, measure, and visualize the data to discuss the issues with equity. These data may involve pedestrian fatalities that disproportionately impact Black, Indigenous, and low-income communities[7] or the fact that access to transportation is important to escaping poverty.[8] We, myself included, have crafted grand plans complete with press conferences committing to making the transportation system safer and improving connectivity. Despite our best efforts to plan, when it is time to implement, we fall short.

As an example, in 2010, Washington, DC, launched the Capital Bikeshare program, which included adding stations in the district's predominately Black wards for the purposes of equity. Despite best efforts, Capital Bikeshare usage was low in the predominately Black wards. At the time, I was a contributor for the regional blog Greater Greater Washington. In a post, I highlighted some of the challenges of bike-share usage in the predominately Black and low-income neighborhoods, such as topography, the fact that membership required a credit card, and the density of stations.[9] In subsequent focus groups exploring low usage, I added the lack of diversity in the advertising, including age, body shape, and perceived socioeconomic status.

In contrast, Philadelphia's bike-share system, Indego, launched in 2015 with a more diverse ridership. It had the advantage of learning from DC and other cities. However, the key to Indego's success is the fact that it centered equity by focusing on people, thanks to funding from The JPB Foundation specifically to build a system on equity.[10] Indego had focus groups where the company received input from Black and low-income people that helped shaped the system, such as having a cash payment option, employment opportunities, and a way to market to their communities. For example, it hired ambassadors from different communities to market and educate their respective communities about the program. And, most important, it made the commitment and budget to invest in and ensure equity.

Both DC's and Philly's systems considered equity, but one focused on place and the other focused on people. As DC continued to analyze why the users lacked diversity, Philly continued to succeed by listening to people and taking action. This is the kind of shift we need in our transportation planning. In chapter 5, I go into more detail on how to include the public in the planning process.

Accelerated Change?

Many of my Black and Brown colleagues who also happen to be my good friends have spoken around the world and written about transportation and equity. We have written papers together.[11] Often, our talks have ended with a round of applause, someone sharing our paper, some tweets quoting something profound that we said, and a few follow-up emails, but nothing changes. We have, though, noticed small changes, including more conference sessions including the word "equity."

However, 2020 brought an accelerated urgency to change that has the transportation industry caught between trying to continue with business as usual and a younger generation willing to push even harder for the industry to evolve. It started off like any other year, but 2020 became a year in which two major events shined a spotlight on race and transportation in a way that we can no longer just applaud and move on with our day. The global pandemic and the protests of police brutality put a huge spotlight on the inequities of the transportation system.

For years to come, the experts will debate when the COVID-19 virus first arrived in the United States, but it was around February 2020 that the reality of an impending global pandemic started to sink in. By March, federal, state, and local governments had started taking swift action by issuing stay-at-home orders. These varied among states, but essentially governments asked people to stay home unless they needed to access an essential service such as food or medicine. Public transit agencies reduced bus and rail to minimum service, and some routes were completely shut down. Grocery stores remained open even as many people relied on grocery delivery services to avoid having to be in public.

People who worked in office settings continued their work at home, tapping away on laptops. Employers converted in-person meetings to online video meetings. Children transitioned to online schooling (I leave discussion of inequities in that to experts in education). As airlines canceled passenger flights and cruise ships docked at ports, the freight industry continued to meet an increased demand for goods as people began to create home offices and places for at-home online schooling. However, many essential workers—people who work in grocery stores, hospitals, pharmacies, and public transit—were left with severely reduced or no public transportation options to get to work.

The pandemic shutdowns also brought to the public spotlight the inequities in communities. Even with a stay-at-home order, people who lived in walkable areas were able to get out of the house during the day and walk to green spaces to meet with friends. It turned out you needed a fairly large park to be able to sit on blankets that were far enough apart to prevent the virus's spread but close enough to have a conversation. However, people in communities that lacked sidewalk infrastructure or parks remained confined to their homes. Empty roads that were already unsafe because of the number of lanes became more unsafe as people drove faster. In 2020, there was an uptick in fatalities, an estimated 23 percent increase for Black people and an 11 percent increase for speed-related crashes.[12] Unfortunately, in 2021 the United States had the highest number of traffic-related fatalities in sixteen years.[13]

The other big defining moment in the first half of 2020 was the focus on police brutality. In May 2020, as the country continued to stay at home, a video of a man named George Floyd started circulating around social media and then mainstream media. Thanks to cellphone video captured by Darnella Frazier, a teenager at the time, we all witnessed a man take his last breath as Derek Chauvin, at the time a police officer, had a knee on George's neck for 8 minutes and 49 seconds in the middle of the public right-of-way. The same public right-of-way where advocates demanded safety from traffic crashes. The country erupted in rage and frustration. Protestors, exercising their First Amendment right to redress grievances with the government, took to the streets—streets that happened to be empty of motor vehicles as people stayed home to prevent the spread of COVID-19.

The momentum of the moment allowed the names of others killed by law enforcement for existing in the public right-of-way to be discussed in social and mainstream media. Elijah McClain, who had been walking home, died from injuries from his interaction with law enforcement that started with a phone call complaining of a "sketchy person" walking on the street. Sandra Bland was pulled over for failure to use her turn signal. Michael Brown was stopped for jaywalking. There are enough examples that Charles T. Brown, a scholar in transportation and owner of Equitable Cities, completed research documenting the overpolicing of Black people within the transportation system, for which he coined the term "arrested mobility." Charles defines arrested mobility as "the direct manifestation of structural racism (racism that is personal, interpersonal, institutional, and cultural), which has led to the intentional and deliberate overpolicing of Black Americans."[14]

The pressure cooker that was the year 2020 also revealed the glaring lack of equity and inclusion in the transportation industry. Local governments advanced Open Streets programs, which entailed closing roads and parking spaces to motor vehicles so restaurants could reopen and maintain six feet of social distance between diners by placing tables in former parking lanes. While some people were enjoying romantic dinners in streets closed by cities, other people protesting police brutality in the same cities were policed for being in the public right-of-way. It led many Black scholars to point out how Open Streets still had their inequities.[15] On one hand, cities made public space available for private use, and on the other hand, cities did not make public space available for public discourse.

From Change to Anger

Newton's third law of motion states that every action has an equal and opposite reaction. As fast as things happened in 2020 to change the conversation in cities across the country, 2021 brought a movement of people pushing back against anything related to equity. If it is associated with diversity, equity, or inclusion, this national movement labeled it "critical race theory" (CRT). Proponents have been quick to attack any mention of a historical event by Black, Indigenous, or other ethnic groups and label it CRT. They labeled conversations about sexual or gender identity as "grooming" young children. All of it fell under the umbrella of "wokeism," a term that co-opted the urban phrase "being woke," meaning being aware, and twisted it to mean something negative. They have taken over school boards and are attacking higher education. Some state legislatures are passing laws making "equity" illegal.

"They" are White nationalists, who unfortunately often cloak themselves with Christian evangelism. Frankly, I do not want to waste many more keystrokes on them. I bring it up to make sure you are aware that they have no desire to see communities reconnected, nor do they care if Black, Brown, or low-income communities are destroyed to make way for new highways and roads.

I did not write this book for them. They do not want to change. I wrote this book for you, but many of you will have to face their opposition.

How to Use This Book

This book is my manifesto: a vision for change and a new era of transportation planning. Much of it is based on my experience as a planner and engineer—the good, the bad, and the meeting that was stopped by the library police—and the lessons I have learned along the way. While it generally focuses on a United States context, mainly because of my experience, the lessons may be applicable to communities in other countries.

My intent is that you do not just read this book and put it back on the shelf, but that you refer to it often as you face different challenges and opportunities. It is a call to action, a practical guide for shaping communities based on principles of justice and equity. Each chapter includes questions for consideration for projects, plans, and studies in your community.

Everyone involved in transportation today has a lot of work to do to repair the injustices of past decisions. Understanding equity in an authentic way is central to changing how we approach and solve problems, make decisions, and create something safer, better, and more useful for all people. Centering people in transportation decisions may sound logical, but it will require a great shift in how we are trained at universities and colleges, the kind of data we collect, how we talk about our projects, and how we work as professional teams—and more. We all use transportation networks, and we can all make them better. Let's start now.

CHAPTER 1

Transportation Is Personal

SOME OF US THINK ABOUT TRANSPORTATION every day because of our profession and interests. However, the reality is that most people do not think about transportation. How they move between an origin and a destination is as routine as breathing. When that routine is disrupted, such as by being delayed by a traffic jam caused by a crash, twisting an ankle on a broken sidewalk, getting a flat tire while riding a bike, or having to stand in unpleasant elements because their bus never arrived—then people notice. Most of the time, they grumble to themselves or repeat the story to whoever will listen. A few will email or tweet their elected representative or whoever they know who works for the municipal government.

Even for those of us nerds immersed in the transportation world, there are elements of transportation that go unnoticed. Throughout my career, I have shared pieces of my story and how I grew up. But I realized how significant reflecting on family history could be when I was on a panel with my friend Justin Garrett Moore, an incredibly accomplished architect. The introduction to his talk included stories about his grandfather and his parents and how they shaped him as a person and a professional.

I realized how powerful it was to acknowledge the influence of family, interwoven with the influence of the places we have lived.

Have you ever reflected on your transportation story? Not just what you do now and why you are passionate about transportation. I am referring to how transportation shaped your life, even when it was that routine thing you did every day and did not think about. As a child, how did you get to school? What were the transportation options in the places where you lived? Was the street a scary place that you avoided, or was it a place where you played with other children in the neighborhood?

What is the role transportation played in your family story?

If you do not work in transportation, you may be less surprised that you have not really thought about these things—but you should. To start to change how transportation networks are created, each of us needs to awaken to the fact that our lives are deeply influenced by these decisions. By being more aware, we can figure out what is working and what needs to change.

As for me, legend has it that I was born into transportation. My dad, who had a thirty-one-year career as a civil engineer and planner, worked for the Federal Transit Administration's predecessor, the Urban Mass Transportation Administration, when I was born. My mom went into labor outside of my dad's office building in Washington, DC. Since this was decades before cell phones, it took some time for my dad's colleagues to alert him that his wife was in the car in labor. Eventually, they found my dad, and my parents made it to the hospital. I was born across the Potomac River in Alexandria, Virginia.

Transportation and Equity Are Encoded in My DNA

On my dad's side, I am the third generation to work in the transportation industry. My paternal grandparents owned the Lincoln Cab Company in Raleigh, North Carolina. In an interview with my grandmother before her passing, she shared that they had as many as thirty-five cabs working for them. My grandmother had been in a car crash, and my grandparents used the insurance money to purchase the cab company. They also had a contract to transport children to school in passenger vans. My few memories of my grandfather are of him coming home from working late driving his cab. When he died, my grandmother sold the company.

Both of my parents were in the transportation field. My dad started his career in the railroad industry. When I was five, we moved from Springfield, Virginia, to Maplewood, New Jersey, because my dad took a job at the Port Authority of New York and New Jersey. Then he worked at SeaLand/CSX at Port Elizabeth in New Jersey. He spent the last thirteen years of his career with the American Society of Civil Engineers (ASCE), serving as the deputy executive director/chief operating officer and the executive director/chief executive officer.

My mom worked for the New York City Transit Authority (NYCTA) for twenty-one years. She worked in human resources, building and overseeing their internship program to recruit new people into public transit. I helped her put together training sessions and traveled around New York City by train with her to meetings. Every day she commuted via public transportation from our small town in New Jersey to Brooklyn. When she first started at NYCTA, she took one train and three subways to get to and from work. Eventually, NJ Transit added service to New York Penn Station, so my mom took an express train from our town to Midtown Manhattan, and then she had one subway ride to Brooklyn.

My sister managed to not follow our parents' career path and became a doctor. However, they instilled in both of us a commitment to uplifting the community. They made sure we understood our family and cultural history as well as making sure we always worked for the betterment of others. My parents often told us the story of how they met while protesting an exhibit on apartheid in South Africa that was being installed and celebrated at their university.

For me, days off from school meant I went to work with one of my parents. At my dad's office, I "oversaw" the shipping operations at Port Elizabeth. At my mom's office, I "trained" interns for their future careers at a public transit agency.

With two parents who had two- to three-hour round-trip commutes to New York City, I spent my weekdays during childhood as a latchkey kid or with nannies and babysitters. It is one reason why as an adult I have always lived within thirty minutes of where I work. Also, the fact that I grew up in a community where I had the freedom to roam, meet friends, play at the playground, and even go to the grocery store by myself is why as an adult I have always lived in a community with access to basic amenities that are accessible without a car. It is also why I am passionate about creating safe transportation infrastructure that a child could navigate independently.

My fellow planner Dan Reed believes communities should be built around children. He calls it the ice cream test, which is the ability of an eight-year-old child to safely get somewhere to buy an ice cream and make it home before it melts. High-comfort bike lanes enable children to bike around safely. Sidewalks, painted crosswalks, and slow traffic enable children to walk or move with a personal mobility device to school, to the playground, or to get ice cream.

Think back to your own childhood. How did the grownups in your life commute to work? How did you get to the grocery store or to school? Do these memories shape how you approach your work in the transportation world, or the decisions you make about where to live, or any other personal decisions?

Transportation Separated My Family

Despite my family having great careers in the transportation industry, we also have a passed-down oral history of how our community was destroyed by transportation. The Louisiana government took my mom's family home and her high school[1] for the construction of a highway in the 1960s. This experience is common to many non-White families in America and yet has been discussed very little for decades.

My mom is from Baton Rouge, Louisiana, which to this day is a racially segregated city. When I was growing up in the 1980s and 1990s, we would visit her family, flying from New Jersey to Louisiana, at least once a year. We would go to my great-grandmother's house for breakfast, which was always a feast. My great-grandmother lived in a humble house that was partially underneath the elevated portion of the Interstate 10 (I-10) highway (figure 1-1). There were no other houses on her block. It was just her home and a corner store.

In her backyard, a massive pillar held up the two-lane ramp above. According to the family stories, every so often vehicles from the highway

Figure 1-1: My mom's brother in front of my great-grandmother's house, where there is now a tree. (Photo provided by the author's mom, Oedies Williams)

would fly off the overpass. My uncle recalled a time when a truck full of cows drove off the highway. I always thought it was strange, but it was not until I was older that I learned how her house ended up under the highway.

Prior to the highway, the block was full of homes owned by Black and Italian families. One of those families was mine. My grandparents lived next to my great-grandmother. The two properties formed an L shape and the backyards connected, making one large backyard. My mom remembers running with her siblings from backyard to backyard. At the corner was a store, which is still there as of the writing of this book. Today, a tree is all that remains of my great-grandmother's property (figure 1-2).

In the 1950s, the State of Louisiana developed a plan to build I-10, which today connects the Florida coast and the California coast. The decision-makers, all White men, settled on going through the

Figure 1-2: Parcel owned by my great-grandmother on Myrtle Avenue (formerly Myrtle Street), shown in 2022. (Photo by Eric Singleton)

underprivileged communities, which were mostly the Black and Italian communities. They took my grandparents' home as well as the others on the block, leaving my great-grandmother's house and the corner store. In addition, prior to the highway, the community had raised money to build a new high school at St. Francis Xavier Roman Catholic Church, which had a majority Black student population. Just four years after the church completed construction of the school, the state tore it down for the highway. My mom was in the last graduating class. As of this writing, a six-lane portion of I-10 still overshadows the church.

I have been unable to find a record of how much Louisiana compensated my grandparents for their home. They ended up moving to another part of town, separated from my great-grandmother. Where my mom's home once stood, there is now a highway pillar (figure 1-3). My family could once walk to church, but the move across the city meant they had to drive to church. Eventually, when I was in elementary

Figure 1-3: My grandparents' house was near the third pillar from the front, looking from East Boulevard in 2022. (Photo by Eric Singleton)

school, my grandparents sold my great-grandmother's property to the corner store and moved her into their home.

I tell this story as a reminder that many communities still have people alive today who remember when the government constructed the highway system, when roads were widened, or when communities were built next to highways. Almost every city in the United States has a highway that either divided a tight-knit community or encircled the community, creating communities segregated by race.[2] Today, these communities are distrustful of the government. We planners and engineers have our work cut out for us, not only to gain trust but also to propose solutions that truly meet the needs of the community. Journalists have a duty to tell the stories of these communities.

Making My Way in the Transportation Field

I am a self-identified transportation nerd. I read anything and everything I can get my hands on related to transportation. Blogs, articles, books, you name it. Even on vacation, I make it a point to use and document my experience with different forms of transportation. I went to Paris, France, and came back with as many photos of transportation infrastructure as photos of tourist areas. Even on my honeymoon in the Cayman Islands, I took photos of the roadway signs. It is always interesting to explore and see how easy or difficult it is to get around in a place that is new to me.

I have decades of experience in transportation planning and engineering with the US Department of Transportation, with local governments, and as a consultant. I have touched major planning projects around the country. Sometimes my touch has had a big influence, such as when I was principal-in-charge for the Vision Zero Action Plans for the District of Columbia and Alexandria, Virginia. Sometimes my touch has been as small as doing a quick hand sketch design on a piece of scrap paper for a protected bike lane in front of my apartment building to prevent the bike lane from being a parking lane.

Three experiences loom large in my life, both professional and personal. In reflecting on them, I hope to broaden our shared understanding of what is critically important for engineers to understand and of the power of representation.

1. How I learned to connect communities and transportation
2. The accidental founding of Black Women Bike
3. Representation or lack thereof in the industry

How I Learned to Connect Communities and Transportation

Despite being more aware than many people of the role transportation can play in our personal lives, it took a college professor and an internship to get me to my "Aha!" moment in learning to connect communities and transportation. As we know, the transportation industry has participated in harm to communities around the country. Plenty of academic books and photos document redlining, segregation, and state departments of transportation that destroyed communities for the creation of the interstate highway system. My parents grew up during the Jim Crow era and keenly remember Whites Only and Coloreds Only signs. My maternal grandfather would drive me around Baton Rouge, pointing out the streets he was not allowed to walk down because his skin was too dark. Frankly, something that happened fifty or sixty years ago seems like a long time ago for me. However, even with the year 2020 feeling like a decade itself, American history is not ancient history.

Many of us in the transportation field see the residual effects of those decisions, including ongoing trauma and impact on the communities now bisected by an unsafe roadway. Even as we attempt to invest in those communities today, resources are often redirected to politically connected and vocal communities—as the saying goes, the squeaky wheel gets the oil.

But even as I reflect on my family history and my upbringing, I credit two people for the influence they had on my career. The first is M. William Sermons, who was my professor in Introduction to Transportation Planning during my junior year of college. He had us review the environmental impact statement (EIS) for Maryland's Intercounty Connector from the lens of a stakeholder. In teams, we had to analyze the document, determine our stakeholder's preferred alternative, and write a position paper. My team focused on the environmentalist stakeholder. Ironically, years later, I was one of the highway engineers for the Final EIS and Record of Decision during my time at the Federal Highway Administration (FHWA).

My takeaway from that class was that civil engineering involves more than just designing roads. It must take into consideration the needs of the community now and in the future, the potential impact of a decision, and the context in which that decision is made. Professor Sermons encouraged me to apply to graduate school and get my master's degree in urban planning.

The second person is Jair Lynch, a real estate developer in Washington, DC. Between undergrad and graduate school, I worked for Jair as an intern. In one of my projects, I worked with the community to develop concepts for recreation centers around DC. The centers were in mostly Black communities that had not received investment for decades. I watched Jair work his magic in community meetings to get people's input. He then worked with the architects to manifest that input in the design. Working with Jair was my first time participating in the planning phase of a project. It was my introduction to working with a community, particularly a community that is not on the same page as the planners for what they want to see in the final report.

A great metaphor that Jair used in determining what would go in the recreation center was going grocery shopping for dinner as a group. We may all have our ideas for what the meal should be, but ultimately we have to stay within a budget. That means we will have to make compromises or choose things that allow for flexibility. The community really connected with the metaphor.

During graduate school, I had a planning class on international development in which the professor dinged our team for not developing a strategy for capacity building. The United Nations defines capacity building as "the process of developing and strengthening the skills, instincts, abilities, processes, and resources that organizations and communities need to survive, adapt, and thrive in a fast-changing world."[3] My team submitted a technically perfect proposal outlining our approach, and with my new enlightenment about engagement thanks to Jair Lynch, we even included community engagement. However, capacity building moves beyond engagement to ask how you are providing resources for the community to continue to expand its work.

What does this look like in a transportation setting? Let's say you are installing a bike lane in a community where one did not exist before. An example of capacity building could be providing the community with a tool kit and resources to host community rides or pop-up clinics to help repair bikes to encourage people to use the bike lane. In addition, you could give them access to appropriate parties to notify when the bike lane requires maintenance, such as sweeping or refreshing the paint. I think many professionals are unclear about this step. We build the bike lane and move on to the next project.

Often, when we are picking classes in college, we think the ones for our major are the most important. Even if college is a distant memory for you, I encourage you to reflect on whether there was a class that influenced how you think about the world in an unexpectedly influential way. For those of you lucky enough to still be choosing classes, I encourage you to be open to serendipity. An anthropology class, of all subjects, was helpful in shaping my career. I am not exactly sure why I enrolled in the class or how I managed to convince my advisors that it was applicable to my planning degree. The value of the class was in learning how to look at communities from a cultural lens. While my planning program was great at teaching us to analyze a community by using census data, it was still a data-focused view of changes in the community over time. However, in my anthropology class, I learned how to understand the culture and the history of the people one is observing. I have found it very helpful in working with communities as I attempt to understand cultures and subcultures within them. The value of this kind of information and interaction needs to be amplified in planning and engineering curricula.

However, even with my love of communities, I admit: there is such a thing as too much community input. I learned this lesson during my time as an urban planner in the Department of Planning and Zoning of the City of Alexandria, Virginia. We did a lot of great engagement for our long-range planning projects. However, our team was focused on attaining a high volume of input rather than targeted input from impacted communities. This approach allowed a very vocal group of citizens who were adept at using the political system to hijack the planning process, often pushing a solution against the will of the impacted communities. For example, we had to change the boundaries of the study area because some of the vocal community members wanted us to remove a playground, claiming that children were making too much noise. Children. At a playground.

The Accidental Founding of Black Women Bike

In 2010, I cofounded Black Women Bike with Najeema Washington and Nse Ufot. It all started when I told them of my experience when biking through a Black community and a little Black girl saw me and was excited. She yelled, "Mommy, there's a Black lady on a bike!" The little girl had seen people on bikes before, but I was the first Black woman she had seen on a bike. Najeema, Nse, and I started talking about the importance of representation in biking. We started using the hashtag #BlackWomenBike.

The founding of Black Women Bike would not have been as significant if there had not also been an existing tension in Washington, DC, at that time. Mayor Adrian Fenty was an avid cyclist and very supportive of bike infrastructure. During his term, the District Department of Transportation installed bike lanes around the city. For some people, bike lanes became a symbol of gentrification and, really, a symbol of young White people moving into Black communities. The bike lanes were seen as symbols of Black communities not getting improvements until White people move in. During the 2010 mayoral race, *Washington Post* journalist Courtland Milloy penned the term "myopic little twits" to represent people who like cupcakes, dog parks, and bike lanes.[4] (As a side note, Courtland also used his national paper platform to write about "bicyclist bullies [who] try to rule the road in D.C."[5] Black Women Bike took him on a ride around DC to experience the city on a bike.[6] It did not make him a bike convert, but he gained a millimeter of understanding.)

Using the name Black Women Bike was our declaration that we exist. The three of us started a Facebook group; within a week, we grew to 64 people, and now, a decade later, there are more than 2,400 Black women in the group. Other Black cycling clubs, such as the Major Taylor Cycling Club, exist. However, our aim was getting Black women on bikes for whatever reason. Regardless of whether it was for exercise, wellness, transportation, or fun, we just wanted Black women on bikes. We also focused on advocacy and education. On the advocacy side, we pushed for better bike infrastructure in our respective neighborhoods, as well as to have at least one member on DC's Bicycle Advisory Council.

For education, we developed a curriculum geared toward getting women biking for transportation. This was aimed at newbies who were getting on a bike for the first time in decades and women who regularly biked for exercise but had never considered biking for transportation. The curriculum even included tips on biking to the grocery store, biking at night, and biking in different types of infrastructure. We attracted and continue to attract women in their forties to sixties, which runs counter to the media narrative that biking is for millennials. For me, biking is freedom—the freedom to come and go when you want and the financial savings from not having to own a vehicle.

Since the founding of Black Women Bike, it has been amazing to see the increase in Black women who are becoming leading voices in the bike community.

Representation or Lack Thereof in the Industry

Building on my experience with Black Women Bike: if you take away one thing from this book, please let it be that representation matters. Does that mean I want to replace White men? No. The work of equity does not fall squarely on the shoulders of Black people, women, queer people, or people with disabilities. If you find yourself uneasy with the direction this topic is leading, please feel welcome to skip to chapter 6 for more discussion and reflection.

In the three decades from the time my dad was a civil engineering undergrad and my own undergrad graduation, the number of women, Black people, and other people of color graduating in civil engineering did not increase significantly. I graduated from the University of Maryland in 2001 with seven other women in a class of thirty students in civil engineering. I was the only Black woman in civil engineering and the only woman who concentrated in transportation.

Even in planning, where women were the majority in my master's program at Cornell University, I was one of two Black people in a class of fifty. We both happened to be women, and colleagues constantly mixed us up simply because of the color of our skin. In my master's in engineering, I was one of two Black people, one of five women, and the only Black woman in a graduating class of one hundred.

Throughout my career as both a planner and an engineer, I have learned to adapt to being the only woman, the only Black person, or the youngest in the room. As the transportation industry navigates conversations about equity and community engagement, I have often been tapped to be the one who leads engagement without being included in the technical processes, despite being perfectly capable of understanding and developing that side of the coin as well.

In 2009, I cofounded Nspiregreen LLC with my good friend Chanceé Lundy. We met through the National Society of Black Engineers, which has a mission for Black engineers to "positively impact the community."[7] Two Black graduate students met on a hot summer day in Brooklyn in 2002 and declared that we would start an engineering company that centered on people. For the eleven years we owned Nspiregreen, we did just that. We fully take credit for the change in the way our clients engaged the community. We changed meeting formats to be more engaging, collected data to understand who was not represented in the public meetings, and got many of our clients to take meetings to where they could find busy people—including bus stops, sidewalks, churches, and rail stations.

Looking back throughout my civil engineering curriculum, I recall that the focus was on design and optimization. Even my undergraduate capstone project was to design a new four-lane roadway in northern Maryland. My team designed our roadway, developed construction costs, and even took care not to go through a cemetery. Looking back now, I can see that the flaw of our capstone was that we never had to hold a single community meeting or even analyze the community. We were engineers given the task of designing a road. This example helps to frame why so many civil engineers struggle with how design impacts the community. My engineering curriculum did not focus on why the road was being designed, only on how to design it and minimize the cost to construct it. When civil engineers are disconnected from the communities where their projects are located, it leads to decisions that prioritize infrastructure over the actual needs of the community. We desperately need to change this.

Within my planning curriculum, I cannot say it was much better. I had a few projects where we had clients, but I did not take any courses that centered on community and *why* we were working with a neighborhood on a plan.

In 2020, I coauthored a paper for the *Carolina Planning Journal* with women whom I respect, tamika l. butler, Anita Cozart, and Dara Baldwin, on the White problem in planning. As Black women, we often become the bridge between worlds. We quoted a portion of "The Bridge Poem" by Kate Rushin, in which the author describes being a bridge between worlds and says "I do more translating / Than the Gawdamn U.N."[8] Our reflection was this:

> Our ancestors passed down the need to protect and nurture, which today means protecting communities of people that look like us. White planners have the privilege of solely focusing on the project or plan, whereas Black women have a constant tension during the plan or project. We know we have to do the technical work based on principles we learned in planning school, but we also have to translate, codeswitch, bridge build, and protect our people. We do more translating than the U.N. and it is exhausting. This need for Black women to do the technical work and emotional labor in this industry is a problem—a white problem.[9]

Even in our success, there is the weight of being the only voice, or one of a few voices, of equity in the room.

My Manifesto

Everyone deserves safe, reliable, and affordable transportation options. By this, I mean that anytime someone needs to get from point A to point B, they have multiple options. I repeat, I am not anti-car. However, I believe strongly that driving in a vehicle alone should not be the default or the only option.

As we look to correct the historical injustices of the transportation system, we cannot use the same tools or the same thinking that disconnected communities. Specifically, this means not building highways and expanding roads that require taking homes and businesses from people. We should not bisect communities, nor should we expand roads to accommodate single-occupancy vehicles.

I do acknowledge there are plenty of places throughout the country that have two-lane roads that are wholly inadequate for the current and future populations. However, roads generally can be expanded without the need to acquire entire properties. Generally, in urban areas, expanding a roadway can mean taking someone's entire property, including their home. In less populated areas, expanding a roadway may mean needing only a few feet of someone's property. In addition, roadway expansion can improve the quality of life for people in less dense areas with sidewalks and other infrastructure; for example, it could connect communities on septic systems within their individual properties to a municipal sanitary sewer system. We just need to think about what most people really need.

I have several goals for writing this book. I hope they are helpful.

Disrupt the Status Quo of the Transportation Industry

We are at a time in history unlike anything experienced by previous generations of engineers and planners. The global pandemic was such a major disruption to life as we knew it that the tools of the past will not be as effective—if they are effective at all.

Prior to the COVID-19 pandemic, only about 6 percent of people in the United States worked from home.[10] In May 2020, almost three months into the pandemic, about 35 percent of people were working remotely.[11] Some companies have implemented permanent telework programs, and others continue to struggle to get their employees to return to the office. Part of what is dubbed "the Great Resignation" is made up of people seeking remote work opportunities.[12] Even as life begins to settle to a new normal, traffic volumes and transit ridership during peak hours have not returned to prepandemic levels in some cities.

We base many transportation decisions on traffic volumes. Currently, we project future traffic volumes using historical trends and using a travel demand model. The specific model inputs and assumptions vary by state and city. The model may account for growth in population and employment. I have seen some travel demand models that assume any new population will move the same as the current population even if people have other options. For example, the model might say that if 1 percent of the population is biking to work today, then 1 percent of people will bike in the future, despite the possibility that new bicycle infrastructure could be added. Not only was that the wrong way of looking to the future before the pandemic, but now, how do we project the new normal of significantly more people telecommuting?

When we project the future on the basis of the past, it leads to overestimating future traffic volumes. The main tool to accommodate the growth in traffic volumes has been expanding roadways to add more lanes. As the transportation adage goes, we cannot build our way out of congestion. Large projects that expand the number of vehicles that can travel are expensive and take decades to design and build. Even researchers acknowledge that expanding the roadways actually increases traffic volumes; this is what is known as induced demand,[13] or, stated in another way, a self-fulfilling prophesy.

Autonomous and electric vehicles are not going to save us if everyone is still alone in the vehicle. Electric vehicles are cleaner, but the industry and state and federal governments have not yet created a holistic means to capture the impact these vehicles will have on the roadways. The gas tax is what funds the national Highway Trust Fund. Since electric vehicles are not using gas, they are not contributing to the trust fund, even though they are using the roadways funded by it. At the most recent conferences I have attended, there still seems to be a misalignment of expectations of autonomous vehicles between the car companies and advocates, particularly the disability and safety advocates. Regardless of all that, if autonomous and electric vehicles do as they predict, all we will achieve is moving congestion more efficiently, with cleaner air.

The larger point is that none of us know the future. If we continue to project from today using trends from the past, we will get the future we predict. My whole goal, which I discuss more in chapter 6, is for you to think about what you want the future to be and then work backward. For example, if you want a future where 80 percent of trips are by public transit, walking, and biking, you need to develop a plan to get there. In contrast, if today you are at only 10 percent and you use the historical growth models, the goal will look different.

Reflect and Elevate

Ongoing acceptance of "This is how we have always done it" continues to harm communities similar to that of my grandparents, who were displaced in the 1960s. In 2022, there are highway projects proposed by state departments of transportation that will remove hundreds of homes and businesses for the sake of added capacity. Many of the same communities still have people living who remember when the state built the highway originally. While it is easy to look at these egregious examples and wag our fingers, this book is a call for personal reflection.

For planners and engineers, this is a call for you to reflect on projects, plans, or policies that you have worked on and to think about the impacts they have had on communities. There will be opportunities to evaluate how you would do things differently. I will share my reflections on projects that did not go as planned and even ones that went well, but I still have my "Wish we would have . . ." moments.

For anyone engaged in advocacy, this is a call for you to look at your coalitions, messaging, and tactics. Do they meet the needs of the communities you are attempting to serve? Are you speaking for them or helping to amplify their voice? Elected leaders will be able to reflect on their actions or inactions. Finally, if you are in a position to write about transportation projects and their effects, it is your duty to interrogate your narratives and language regarding transportation projects. Are you still using the passive voice, saying "A car hit a person walking down the street," or do you refer to the person who performed the action—the driver? Are they accidents, crashes, or traffic violence? There has been a lot of rich conversation about how the way we write about issues can obscure the truth or make it more palatable. It is time to change.

This book is a request for you to elevate your consciousness. Not in a way that is performative or even overly apologetic. It requires you to build empathy for communities regardless of your role in the decision-making process. Then, once you unlock that consciousness, evaluate how you will be better and do better.

Keep Us Focused on the Little Things with Major Impacts

As technology and the world continue to change, there will still be the last-mile and, in some cases, last-few-feet connections. I am by no means anti-technology. I love how applications have evolved such that from the phone in your hand you can pay your transit fare and know when the next bus is coming. The next generation of applications promises the ability to plan travel using multiple modes, for example, using a bike share to transit and then walking the rest of the way.

However, all the widgets and gadgets are no substitute for people's ability to move on their own by walking; by using a device that assists them with moving, such as a wheelchair or a rolling walker; or by riding a bicycle. The bicycle was invented almost four hundred years before the first automobile. As technologies have come and gone, the bicycle has remained. I think some of the best technologies enhance these choices, such as the applications I mentioned, rather than revolutionize the entire system. E-bikes are a great example because they allow new riders who are physically unable to ride long distances to participate in that mode of transportation. Transit applications on the phone provide real-time information on the location of buses, trains, and so forth, and when the next one will arrive.

I used the term "last-mile connection" and expanded it to "last-few-feet connection," which refers to a gap in the transportation network. For example, an autonomous, on-demand mode of transit may get people to a bus stop near where they work or live. However, are they able to get from where they live to the bus stop? In addition, there will be trips of only one or two blocks that are easier to walk or use a device that assists people with moving. And sometimes it is just as simple as people liking to move without being in a vehicle.

We cannot allow technology to distract us from the need to create safe, affordable communities where people can walk, wheel, or bike short distances to meet their basic needs. This means streets with plenty of space to move, trees to shade, and places to take a break. In many cities, it means reclaiming space that is currently dedicated to moving or storing motor vehicles.

Give You More than an Idea or a Catchphrase

One of the books I keep on my nightstand is *Think and Grow Rich* by Napoleon Hill. What I love about the book, beyond the great information it provides, is that it includes questions for reflection and actionable steps. That is my goal. To give you a book that you can read from cover to cover or skip around in based on your interest, underline, and tab for future reference. Some ideas may seem repetitive, but my aim is for you to be able to refer back to pieces and still have the context.

In the end, I hope you will use this book to improve how you approach your work, whether it be a project, a plan, a policy, a grassroots campaign, or even an opinion piece.

Pause for Reflection

While sharing my personal transportation story, I invited you to think about yours. Take a moment to write your transportation story. How has your history shaped who you are today? Think about where you lived, how you spent time getting around, and how that affected your days. Beyond your résumé, who are you? How does transportation play a role in this? What is your view of what the future of transportation could be?

CHAPTER 2

Equity Is More than a Baseball Graphic

WHETHER YOU ARE WELL VERSED IN EQUITY, still learning, or completely skeptical, this is an important chapter to read. Equity is the foundation for the rest of the book—just as it should be the foundation of transportation plans. Even if after this chapter we still do not have a shared understanding of equity, the information in this chapter offers insight into my experiences, thoughts, and reflections referred to in the rest of the book.

"Transportation planning decisions often have significant equity impacts," wrote Todd Litman of the Victoria Transport Policy Institute, an independent research organization. "Transport equity analysis can be difficult because there are several types of equity, many potential impacts to consider, various ways to measure impacts, and many possible ways to categorize people."[1] Often, equity will reflect the values of the community, and therefore it is impossible to have a basic checklist and achieve something meaningful.

Before I jump in, take five minutes and write down your definition of equity. Try not to overthink it. A paragraph definition, bullet points, or word art are all acceptable ways to note your definition.

All done? Great; put it aside, and we will come back to it at the end of the chapter.

There are three goals for this chapter. One, to establish the outdated concept of equality versus equity and why it is harmful. Two, to hold the somewhat better idea of equity up and then poke some holes in it. Finally, to lay the groundwork for how to think about the meaning behind these words in a way that helps you incorporate this understanding into your work.

Do you remember when you first encountered the term "equity" in a context that had nothing to do with finance?

For me, somewhere between 2016 and 2018, I noticed "equity" was occurring more frequently in conference titles, descriptions, and presentations. In these presentations, the speakers showed the numbers they crunched and fancy maps to tell us what we already knew—Black, Brown, and low-income communities lack connectivity, the people in those communities have poor health outcomes, and their neighborhoods today reflect decades of disinvestment. In presentation after presentation, there was something missing from the discussion. Mainly, what do we need to do so these communities have better connectivity and health outcomes?

I recall that before I first noticed the term's frequent appearance, we had some brief readings about equity in planning school. I read probably one of the first writings on justice and transportation with a US focus, a book edited by Robert Bullard and Glenn Johnson titled *Just Transportation: Dismantling Race and Class Barriers to Mobility*, published in 1997. Generally, outside of a couple of books and a handful of academic papers, the transportation industry was silent about equity until the mid-2010s. Around that time, several books discussing transportation and equity were introduced. Some focused on a specific mode, such as biking or public transportation.

Equality versus Equity: An Outdated Concept—Baseball

Whether in a book or a presentation, everyone tries to explain or define equity. You have probably seen different graphics that try to illustrate the difference between equality and equity. The most used graphic shows three people of different heights trying to see over a fence to watch a baseball game (figure 2-1). To depict equality, each person has a box of the same height. The tall person can see over the fence, but the boxes are not high enough for the two shorter people to see over the fence. The caption generally reads something like "Equality means everyone gets the same."

The graphic depicting equity shows each person having an appropriately sized box so that they can all see over the fence. The shorter person has the tallest box, and the taller person has the shortest box (or, in some versions of the graphic, they do not have a box because they do not need it to see over the fence). The accompanying text is "Equity means everyone gets what they need."

Despite my current critique, I openly admit I have used some variations of this graphic. I have even taken it further to say that equity means giving people what they need rather than what you think they need. It is not a wrong statement, but from a graphic perspective it assumes I believe they need to see the game, when in fact they may have different needs altogether. In trying to create a simple graphic to explain two words that are similar in meaning, there is still room for opposing interpretations.

One interpretation by scholar tamika l. butler, adapted from a presentation by Vedette Gavin, points out, "There's still someone who has decided that the goal of these folks is to watch a baseball game. But what if you don't like baseball? What if you want to play in the game? What if you want to coach the team? What if you want to own the

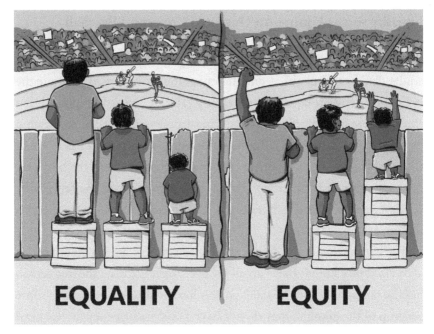

Figure 2-1: Popular illustration of equity (right) versus equality (left) showing three individuals trying to watch a baseball game.
(Interaction Institute for Social Change | Artist: Angus Maguire)

team? What if you want to be the business person that has an exclusive contract with the stadium and you're providing all the food?"[2] tamika's view is that the image misses the underlying concepts of power and who holds the power.

An opposing interpretation of equity is that it means taking from someone to give to someone else. In a civil engineering forum that I am part of, someone posted the baseball graphic. One person commented that the tall person had to give away their box to the shortest person so the shortest person could see over the fence. They likened it to socialism, since scarce resources were being redistributed. In all the times I have seen the graphic, this was my first time hearing this interpretation. I went back and looked at the graphic and yes, in one commonly distributed version, the tall person does give their box to the shortest person. However, the "socialist" interpretation completely ignores that the tall person does not need the box to see the game. Some communities have such a high need from decades of disinvestment that they need the resources meant for another neighborhood.

Another interpretation from the same engineering forum was that all three people were stealing because they did not pay for tickets to see the game. Since none of them had the resources to purchase tickets, none of them deserved to see the game. These extreme views of the graphic distract from its intent of explaining equity versus equality.

An illustration from the Robert Wood Johnson Foundation tackles equity and equality by showing people on different types of bicycles (figure 2-2). Equality is illustrated by people of various heights and abilities or disabilities on bicycles of the same size; equity is represented by everyone on a bike of the appropriate size and type for them. This visually fits with what the transportation industry generally accepts as the definition of equity: everyone getting what they need.

Figure 2-2: Illustration of equity versus equality using individuals on bicycles. (Robert Wood Johnson Foundation, #PromoteHealthEquity)

Every transportation project starts with the need, which should clearly articulate why the project is being planned, studied, or evaluated. The need informs the purpose, and the purpose informs the potential solutions. Data will provide some insight into what the community may need. As stated earlier, data can reflect the bias of the person who is collecting and analyzing it. However, the lived experience of the community is an important data point. Equity starts with an inclusive outreach process to understand what is the community's need rather than what you may interpret as the need.

Okay, but What *Is* "Equity"?

For a seemingly straightforward definition of equity, we could turn to Merriam-Webster's dictionary, which defines equity as "justice according to natural law or right."[3] It is interesting that in defining equity for transportation purposes, the "justice" gets lost. In the case of transportation, what would be the natural law or right? Some may define it as owning a car to have the freedom to go where you want and when you want. Others may define it as the right to a clean environment and transportation options.

The New York State Transportation Equity Alliance, a coalition of groups across the state, says that "equitable transportation is people-centered, protects our health and communities, prioritizes sustainability, gives everyone a voice in the planning process and is the underpinning of a vibrant economy."[4] The Victoria Transport Policy Institute defines equity as "the fairness with which impacts (benefits and costs) are distributed."[5]

Some academics have abandoned the term "equity" altogether in favor of "justice." Setha Low, a professor at the City University of New York, defines justice as distributive, procedural, and interactional. Distributive justice would ensure that all public space is available to all people.

For example, are we being just in how we allocate the right-of-way to all of the people who need to move, or have we made a roadway only for people in cars? Procedural justice is about fairness and the ability to influence decision-making. Is the public engagement process transparent, and is everyone heard? Interactional justice is about people feeling welcome in the public space.[6] Are people being harassed for being in the public space, or is it truly welcoming to everyone?

There are other variations of the definition of equity and what it means for transportation. Phrasing aside, it all comes down to a vision of fairness and communities having what they need. The fundamental challenge is that the needs of the community more than likely exceed the resources available at any given time.

The Fundamental Problem with Equity

Whether it is a report, policy paper, or conference presentation, the definition is less important than the action or inaction behind it. What I have seen in my career is that communities expend effort developing transportation equity plans, but when it is time to implement, the community divides the resource pie so everyone's neighborhood gets some incremental change. However, that incremental change is not enough to make a noticeable difference. The areas that need it most never get the resources they need.

The reality is that equity demands we make hard decisions to prioritize resources—people, time, and money. For governments, this can be challenging. It requires elected leadership willing to make the hard decisions and a transportation department willing to implement them. Elected leaders want to get reelected, so they will push for resources for their constituents even when they do not have the greatest need. Richer communities will point out that their tax dollars are funding the improvement, so they should get the resources in their community.

Without a true commitment to equity, the allocation of resources gets decided by who attends the public meetings, who has influence over the decision-making process and the people making the decision, and, more important, who has the power at the expense of the Silently Suffering (see chapter 4).

When I look at my experiences being a woman, being Black, and being a planner and engineer in the transportation industry, I realize that the largest barrier to equity is leadership. Elected leaders, heads of transportation agencies, principals at consultant firms, directors of advocacy groups, and editors of newspapers all have to be committed to equity. That means commitment in the face of adversity. It means being intentional regarding decisions.

One project I worked on was to navigate the decision-making process by developing a framework for equity. The goal was to have a data-driven process for allocating resources to improve safety.

Case Study: An Equity Framework for Vision Zero

In 2019, I was one of the consultants working with Montgomery County, Maryland, on its Vision Zero Equity Framework to achieve its overall goal of zero traffic-related deaths and serious injuries. The county's data analysis showed that its high injury network was mostly in communities with high percentages of Black, Latino, and immigrant people, low-income communities, or both. Working with a task force of about twenty citizens, we developed a framework.

I will admit the task force lacked diversity. In general, we had some geographic diversity, although the majority of members lived in the denser areas of the county, and gender diversity. We had one high school student and one person who was visually impaired. However, the task force did not represent the racial, ethnic, or age diversity of

Montgomery County. Despite that, members of the task force worked together to develop a framework for equity.

How We Started

We asked the question "What does equity look like if we can achieve it?" If we had asked people to define equity, we would have ended up with a generic definition of "everybody gets what they need." The root of our question was how to know when you have achieved equity. The task force responded with some great descriptions, such as "Each community's roads and sidewalks have features that are adapted to the specific characteristics of those communities and enable safe mobility."

Next, the county staff showed data indicating that people were dying in the equity emphasis areas, which the Metropolitan Washington Council of Governments defined as areas with high concentrations of Black, immigrant, and low-income communities. The task force members agreed that this was horrible and the transportation department should concentrate the Vision Zero resources in these areas. However, as soon as we moderated a conversation about the allocation of money, the conversation changed. Constraining resources often leads to people feeling the need to advocate for their specific community.

When we started discussing money, at the beginning of the conversation there was a complaint, or rather a perception, that the rich areas were getting all the resources. Given the data, that was not an accurate statement. When asked how to spend Vision Zero resources, some members of the task force defaulted to their community as a priority, which, again based on data, did not have the greatest need. This highlights the fundamental issue of equity. We can all agree that it is horrible that things are inequitable. However, when communities have limited resources, there is an instinct to make the case for one's own community.

How We Got People Out of the Rut

We reframed equity as prioritization. The analogy I came up with was an emergency room (ER). Each emergency department has a decision process that determines the order in which doctors and nurses attend to patients, as well as who gets admitted to the hospital and who gets discharged. When a person arrives at the ER, the intake nurses assess their condition and take their vital signs. Theoretically, a patient's income, health insurance status, and race or ethnicity do not impact where they fall on the priority list. Generally, patients are seen in order of arrival, but someone who comes in with a more serious condition supersedes anyone who was there first.

For example, when my daughter was six months old, my husband and I took her to a pediatric urgent care clinic because she had a severe allergic reaction. When we arrived, there were children with runny noses and coughs in the waiting room. The intake nurse assessed my daughter and determined that she was experiencing anaphylaxis. Even though we had just arrived, they brought her to an examination room immediately. The nurse said loudly, "Redbox," and all the doctors and nurses left the patients they were seeing in other exam rooms to get to my daughter's side. At that moment, she was the patient with the greatest need and required the most resources. Even though she was the most recent arrival, she was placed at the front of the line because her condition was the most critical. Once they had administered medicine and she was stable, the doctors and nurses returned to the other children.

This is what equity is about.

Similar to the prioritization in an ER, there is always room for improvement in every transportation network, and people's transportation concerns may be addressed eventually. But some communities (those with high fatality statistics, for example) require immediate attention and resources in order to be stabilized. In some cases, they need additional continuous attention, as do ER patients who are admitted to the hospital. Data will show that some communities are in critical condition because they have an overburden of roads on the high injury network, roads in poor conditions, and high negative public health impacts such as asthma. As with my daughter's trip to the ER, these communities need a concentration of resources (money, staff time, projects) to get them stabilized. They should be the highest priority (figure 2-3).

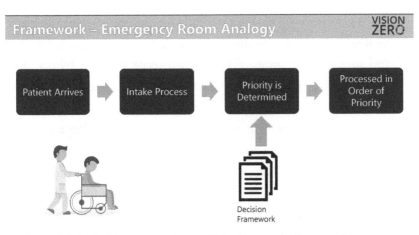

Figure 2-3: In the Montgomery County Vision Zero Equity Framework, we use an emergency room to provide an example of equity.

End Result

In the end, we never developed a definition of equity. We ended up with guiding principles to help the county prioritize communities with the greatest need.

Montgomery County's guiding principles are as follows:

- Community Engagement: Montgomery County will consider everyone's voices and concerns, which includes being proactive to engage communities that may not be currently represented in the process or make requests for safety projects.

- Access: Residents all over Montgomery County can safely access multiple transportation options to reach their destination.
- High Injury Network: Using a data-informed approach, Montgomery County will prioritize funding to the high injury network, with special attention to equity emphasis areas as defined by the Metropolitan Washington Council of Governments and shown in the Vision Zero Two-Year Action Plan.
- Address Historical Disinvestment: Montgomery County will invest in areas that are historically underserved by transportation funding and projects that improve safety for people walking, biking, and using mobility assistive equipment (wheelchair, canes, etc.).[7]

Montgomery County is using this framework to develop a ten-year Vision Zero plan as well as a guide for where to spend capital improvement dollars. What this means in practical terms is that the county is programming its resources to go first to the communities that need them the most, which is a shift from giving the resources on a first-come, first-served basis or, worse, giving the resources to the squeaky wheels. As other resources become available over time, they will go to the other areas in the county.

Restoration

The word "equity" has lost its meaning among planners and engineers. It has been reduced to a map or an analysis. In the wake of 2020, consultants, governments, elected leaders, advocates, and journalists are in a rush to "do the equity," and many are getting stuck in the paralysis of analysis. For example, elected leaders are still reluctant to reallocate road space to bicyclists because of pushback from community members who say they will not be able to drive as fast. In lieu of a decision, there is procrastination in the form of more public engagement or additional analysis. As I reflect on my personal and professional experiences, equity analysis is not enough. It is not even the bare minimum.

Also, as I mentioned in the previous chapter, there are people actively fighting against "equity." No one can pinpoint the original author, but a popular internet quote is "When you are accustomed to privilege, equity can feel like oppression." In the view of the tall person in the equity graphic who is giving up their box to the shortest person, it can feel like the tall person was unfairly punished. As stated previously, it ignores the fact that the tall person already had the privilege of being able to see over the fence and did not need the box. Creating a space for other modes of travel is an attempt by the government to forcibly reduce people's right to drive as fast as they please.

Not that this will ever sway the people who react allergically to any occurrence of the word "equity," but another, less rote way of looking at equity is in terms of restoration. This may in fact be a good step toward developing new ways of planning and project development that better address past harms. In some cases, restoration looks drastic, such as removing or capping a highway that creates a barrier in the community. In others, it may be as simple as repairing a road full of potholes and adding a stop sign. The key in this approach is that it is critical to understand the past harms. It connects cultural anthropology, you might say, to present-day outreach and decision-making.

PolicyLink, a national research action institute, developed an equity manifesto. An equity manifesto can play the same role as guiding principles if it appeals more to your community. PolicyLink's manifesto states, "[Equity] requires that we understand the past, without being trapped in it; embrace the present, without being constrained by it; and look to the future, guided by the hopes and courage of those who have fought before and beside us."[8] In chapter 5, I will discuss in more depth how to use history to shape the future. But the reflection here is that without understanding past harms, we can repeat them in the future.

Similarly, People for Mobility Justice defines equity much more closely to the analogy of an ER, without quite saying it: "correcting past discrimination in how public transportation benefits and burdens are allocated, maintained, and developed. Those who have had the least should be given the most. Mobility justice includes holding government agencies accountable to the principles they have set out in defining transportation equity and related topics such as environmental justice and transit justice."[9]

Restoration is about more than checking the Engagement box. It is about acknowledging the past and providing a path forward, which means spending time to understand what has happened in the past. In the next chapter, I will talk more about going beyond the traditional existing conditions analysis to engage the community and recognize past harms to that community—neglect of a community is as harmful as an overburden of traffic. Restoration looks like working with the community to develop a vision for moving forward and providing the necessary resources to bring that to fruition.

For communities that were historically traumatized by the transportation system and that continue to be neglected, transportation planning and projects should prioritize restoration and justice. Specifically, this looks like investing resources in those communities first to ensure they have what they need to be stable.

Opportunity for Reflection: Developing Your Framework

Pull out that definition I asked you to write at the beginning of the chapter. Take two minutes to review and make any edits. Did your definition change?

You made it this far to realize that I did not provide you with a definition of equity. But I think definitions are a trap. As my experience in Montgomery County shows, you can spin your wheels trying to come up with a definition. Particularly, that definition may change depending on the context and values in a community. If your community has a Vision Zero plan, then there is a set value, that people should not die in a traffic-related incident, that will guide your equity framework.

As you think about a project that you may be working on or that may be underway in your community, reflect on the ER example. Whether you want to call it guiding principles or something else, you essentially need a decision framework that determines the order in which communities are addressed and which ones get more attention and resources.

1. Let the Data Guide You

Let's say you have a program like Vision Zero, where you are trying to eliminate traffic-related fatalities and serious injuries. The first step is mapping the crash data to see where these types of crashes are occurring. Are the crashes clustered in certain parts of the community, or are they all over? What are the demographic profiles of the communities where the crashes are occurring?

Another example could be a sidewalk program. Map all the existing sidewalks on one or both sides of the street. If you have the data, you can also map the condition of the sidewalks. Which communities have no sidewalks or have sidewalks that are in poor condition? What are the demographics of those communities?

Next, and frankly the hard part for communities: how is the program money being spent today? Is the money evenly distributed around the community or clustered in certain areas? How is the money being invested, and where are the areas with the greatest need?

For community advocates and journalists, you may need to submit a Freedom of Information Act request to get these data. Also, be prepared to contextualize the information. For example, is the program first come, first served; does each political boundary receive an allotment; or is there some combination of both? Is it by request, and are certain communities more diligent, or do they have more time to make requests?

2. What Does Equity Look Like if You Achieve It?

The response to this question is the basis for the decision framework. Once you complete step 1, you will have a baseline understanding of where there are problems and how the money is being spent in the present. This is a great step in which to engage different stakeholders and communities, especially the ones most affected by inaction. Present them with the data and the need as you understand it. Then engage them in a conversation about their needs as they see them. For example, the data may say that people are being struck and killed at a midblock crossing. The community may be able to provide context for why people are crossing there. Is it the shortest path to get to the bus stop, grocery store, or another place where people are trying to go?

Note to anyone interviewing community members: probe their answers. Ask them to clarify what they mean when they describe what equity looks like if achieved. "Why" questions are great ways to dig deeper. Make no assumptions!

3. Develop Guiding Principles

With what you learned in step 2, draft some guiding principles. Essentially, these are the big picture descriptions of how you will get from where you are today to the vision of what equity looks like if it is achieved. In the Montgomery County example, the guiding principle to prioritize the high injury network provides the framework to put resources in the areas with the greatest need.

This is a second place to do stakeholder engagement that includes elected and agency leadership. If the new principles are the guardrails for how resources are allocated, the leadership needs to understand that when a neighborhood falls outside of those parameters, it will go on the list for improvements, but it will have to wait until the priority areas are addressed. This is hard, especially when there are vocal advocates for business as usual—spending money where it has always been spent, or where people pay higher taxes, and so on. Leadership will need to have the fortitude to stay the course and stay within the guiding principles.

.

CHAPTER 3

Should There Be a War on Cars?

ON APRIL 27, 1996, I GOT MY FIRST DRIVER'S LICENSE. It is a milestone date in my life I will always remember. In my seventeen-year-old brain (do not do the math), it was my ticket to true independence. For my mom, it meant not having to figure out how to get me to my sports practices or dance classes after a long day of work. One month after I got my license, my dad bought me my first car, which was a 1996 Dodge Neon because he saw the ad that said "Hi." I will admit, the car did look like it was smiling. The Neon and I had many adventures and misadventures, like the time I spun out on the highway because I was driving too fast.

Cars are as American as apple pie. More important, they are a symbol of freedom. If I own a car, I can go wherever I want, whenever I want, and as fast as I want, assuming there is no law enforcement around. People in the United States have a love affair with cars. It is part of our culture. Cars are a status symbol. The car you drive allows others to assess what they think is your wealth. It allows people to discern whether you are "one of us" or you are "not from around these parts." Car company ads market to us a lifestyle.

That, my friends, is the problem. Cars. But you may be thinking, "You said you were not anti-car, and now you are saying cars are the problem?" Correct. I am not anti-car, and yes, cars are the problem. Prioritizing cars creates traffic congestion. Whether I love or hate cars, the fact remains that they are not efficient ways to move people. Think about it this way: fifty people driving alone will take up more roadway space than fifty people on a bus, on bicycles, or on the sidewalk. Traffic-related deaths and serious injuries are caused by people driving cars, and the fact is that the existing transportation system is overbuilt, trying to alleviate congestion during commute periods so people can have the freedom to drive to work in their cars by themselves. As a result of this effort to alleviate traffic congestion during commute periods, the near-empty roads during nonpeak times enable people to drive at unsafe speeds—thus, fatalities in motor vehicle crashes are a leading cause of death in the United States.[1]

Additional problems are caused by the transportation industry, such as poor air quality and the societal cost of motor vehicle crashes.[2] The transportation sector accounts for 27 percent of greenhouse gas emissions, which impact climate change.[3] What about the fact that 43 percent of the roadway system is in poor or mediocre condition?[4] At the root of the root, it is still cars causing problems. Transportation dollars are spent by state and local departments of transportation for expanding highways and roadways to alleviate congestion for people in cars, with minimal dollars available for maintenance of roads destroyed by cars.

While we are on the topic of cars, surface parking lots—which I realize are not in the public right-of-way—and on-street parking are some of the biggest wastes of space. Parking lots are generally large seas of asphalt that contribute to stormwater runoff and the heat island effect, and they are almost always empty. As malls continue to meet their demise around the country, some are being repurposed as residential developments and others are demolished to make way for a denser town center. Land is more valuable as a dense development with retail, office, and residential spaces than it is as a surface parking lot. Dense developments generate tax revenue, while parking lots are parking lots. The pandemic showed us that on-street parking spaces provided more economic benefit as outdoor restaurant seating than as all-day storage for cars.

Not to oversimplify the problems of transportation, but all roads lead back to cars, no pun intended.

Traffic Congestion—How Did We Get into This Mess?

Most major metropolitan areas have traffic congestion as people commute into the central business district (CBD) for work in the mornings and out of the CBD to go home in the evenings. Before the introduction of the motor vehicle, most downtowns in the United States were thriving metropolises because people lived, worked, and played downtown. Even cities that today we say are car-centric, such as Los Angeles and Detroit, were designed around moving people efficiently. As a matter of fact, in the 1920s, Los Angeles had one of the most robust streetcar networks.[5] If you examine historical photos of downtowns, you will see horse-drawn buggies, dense streetcar networks, and wide sidewalks. More importantly, you will see people. Today, some downtowns die around six o'clock in the evening as commuters make their escape to the suburbs.

The urban renewal of the 1950s through 1960s was probably one of the most destructive times in the history of American cities. Entire neighborhoods, including vibrant downtowns, were leveled to create something "new." Our predecessors designed and built a car-centric transportation system. The car, the status symbol, could carry you to your new suburban home. Well, if you were White. To accommodate the traffic, neighborhoods, mostly Black, low income, or both, were bulldozed by federal, state, and local governments to build wide roads.

Designing around the car has been detrimental to people and the environment. Roads that once had wide sidewalks are today hostile to people walking, in order to accommodate more cars. These same roads often lack sidewalks and curb ramps that would make them accessible for people using a wheelchair or pushing a stroller. How we built the environment is why transportation systems are one of the social determinants of health. For example, a lack of sidewalks is a barrier to active transportation, which researchers have linked to childhood obesity.[6] Back in the day, children walked to school, playgrounds, and other destinations, like libraries, because there was little risk of being struck by a car. The inverse is also true. If people use motor vehicles less, it can improve health outcomes.[7]

The Numbers—Level of Service by Its Nature Leads to Widening Roadways

Most engineers first encounter the term "level of service" (LOS) in the junior year of their undergraduate program. Planners may or may not hear about it until graduate school. People in policy, politics, and journalism understand it insofar as a grade of A is good and F is bad.

LOS at its most basic is a measure of the volume of vehicles on a roadway versus the capacity of the roadway. The equation is LOS $= v/c$.[8] When the volume exceeds the capacity, the vehicles are stuck in gridlock. It gets a grade of F, meaning it fails, and someone stuck in that gridlock is sending their elected official an angry email or posting on social media. When the volume is significantly below the capacity, people can drive unimpeded. This gets a grade of A, which is misinterpreted to mean it is what we should achieve. When people can drive unimpeded, what do they do? They speed.

The grading system, from A being free-flowing to F being gridlock, is used by engineers and planners to communicate with the public and elected officials. One problem is that people being stuck in traffic leads to political pressure to "fix the problem." And then, perhaps more critically, no one likes the grade F because anyone knows it is associated with failure. Basically, the LOS grading system is a clear way to communicate but has the unintended side effect of making it seem that the whole goal is to achieve an A for this one metric. Decision-makers get it in their mind that any traffic flow that gets worse is unacceptable, even if it means adding a bus-only lane or a protected bicycle lane, which can move more people. And a lot of negative side effects come with seeing road expansion as your only option to reduce congestion, as I have pointed out.

With LOS as the guiding principle, naturally the solving of congestion focuses on peak times, which are the morning and evening rush hours. Our predecessors designed roads for the worst six or so hours of the day—and the business as usual approach continues this practice even now. During the other eighteen or so hours, however, the roads have excess capacity, which leads to people speeding, which in turn leads to a high number of crashes. It is dangerous, and wasteful, similar to how big-box retailers build surface parking lots for Black Friday shopping, and for the rest of the year these lots are virtually empty.[9]

This A–F approach leaves transportation planners and engineers with two options. Either decrease the volume of vehicles, such as by increasing public transit and high-occupancy vehicle (HOV) lanes, or increase the capacity of the roadway, such as by improving operations or expanding. The most economical solution is to improve operations by changing signal timing, utilizing incident management to quickly clear crashes, and providing real-time traveler data so drivers can make different travel decisions.

For decades, the solution to congestion has been to add more lanes to the roadway, which increases capacity and allows a higher volume of cars to move. The outcome is wide highways and roads that are dangerous from safety and public health perspectives. Some state departments of transportation have repurposed general travel lanes for HOV lanes, high-occupancy toll (HOT) lanes, and managed lanes. The goals of these are to encourage people to carpool to reduce the number of cars on the highway, which is a good thing. Quick aside: the Virginia Department of Transportation introduced HOV lanes in the early 1970s, which led to the cultural phenomenon called "slugging," in which strangers ride together to reach the minimum number of people needed to use the HOV lanes. At park and rides all around northern Virginia, at least two strangers going to the same destination will hop into the car of a third stranger so all three can take advantage of riding the HOV lane into Washington, DC.[10]

However, even with HOV lanes, toll lanes, and congestion pricing, which allows the toll price to fluctuate with traffic, and as we have become more enlightened regarding other modes of transportation that move more people efficiently, the state departments of transportation are spending billions nationwide to widen roadways. For example, the State of Louisiana is proposing to invest $1.1 billion to widen the same Interstate 10 that destroyed my family's neighborhood in Baton Rouge. In February 2021, through the environmental review process established by the National Environmental Policy Act, the state received a Finding of No Significant Impact (FONSI) despite the need to acquire twenty-seven residential and five commercial structures, of which 64 percent are in environmental justice communities, defined as communities made up mostly of people of color and low income.[11] Depending on your point of view, you may or may not agree with the assessment that acquiring twenty-seven residential properties is not significant.

However, how much should a community have to endure? Especially when the $1.1 billion could have gone toward $15 billion in deferred maintenance.[12] For nonengineers, this would be equivalent to adding another room to a house while ignoring a leaking roof. They are building more roads even though they have miles of roads that are aging and in need of repair. While federal money has certain restrictions, as a country we continue to fund expansion at the expense of maintenance. My cynical side says that one explanation is that there are no ribbon cuttings and photo opportunities for a newly repaved road.

But Let's Address the Elephant in the Room: Racism and Lack of Diversity

I waited until chapter 3, but let us discuss. No, highways and roadways are not racists. Highways are inanimate objects. However. Historically, the transportation industry lacked diversity at the decision-making levels. In the 1950s and 1960s, when the highway system was planned, designed, and constructed, racism was embedded in the process.

The invention of the automobile, along with government housing loans for White veterans, eventually led to the creation of suburban housing, creating White flight to those suburbs to achieve the American Dream of a house with a yard and a garage for the car. An interesting thing is that if you do an internet search on "American Dream ads," you'll notice that they all show a White family made up of a mom, a dad, a boy, a girl, and a pet. Either they are outside their house, with a white picket fence and their motor vehicle in the driveway, or they are in their motor vehicle. The sprawling growth of the suburban and exurban areas for living—while people still needed to commute downtown for work—led to the perceived need for more roads.

In those days, the people making decisions regarding highways were White men. Engineers and planners intentionally designed the national highway system to go through Black, Brown, and low-income neighborhoods.[13] There were some attempts to build them through White neighborhoods, but these were often met with resistance from those communities. Putting the highways through Black, Brown, and low-income neighborhoods was the path of least resistance. Not because people in those communities did not care—but because they had the least power. Black people did not have the right to vote until 1965, so technically they were not a political threat.

While I did state that I was not going to go too deeply into history that is documented by others, I do want to make sure one thing is clear. Racism shaped the urban and suburban areas, where even today we see the residual effects. For the United States, this period was during the Jim Crow era and the beginnings of the civil rights movement. In the land use context, restrictions were imposed on who could live in what community via deed restrictions, protective covenants, redlining, and, more subtly, marketing by real estate agents.[14] Deed restrictions were explicit to Black people and others deemed non-White, which during that time included people who were Irish, Italian, and Jewish. (Even though these restrictions are not legally enforceable, they still show up on deeds.)[15]

In transportation, this shows up in disproportionate impacts on communities today. Across the United States, Black, Latino, and Indigenous communities are overrepresented in pedestrian fatalities,[16] asthma,[17] heart disease, and obesity.[18] There are plenty of "get out and move" campaigns, but how does one get out and move when there are no sidewalks or paths, no trees to provide shade, and no places to sit when one gets tired? Even active transportation falls flat when there are no safe places to bike to grocery stores, jobs, places of worship, and schools, or places to lock your bike once you arrive. Improving health outcomes in many of these communities will require more than encouraging behavioral changes. It will require acknowledging and correcting the systemic racism that has shaped the physical infrastructure. If you think back to chapter 2, you'll recall that the data show these are clearly the populations around the country that have the most need for investment.

While the industry has improved since the 1960s, it continues to lack diversity at the decision-making levels in transportation agencies and consultant teams. This means people making the decisions may have never personally lived with the impacts of past harm caused by transportation—and that makes a real difference in how you think about the problem. Without a focused effort to put resources into the areas with the highest needs, those communities will continue to experience higher traffic-related fatalities and poor health outcomes.

A New Way of Thinking

It is easy to critique our predecessors because we have the benefit of knowing the outcome, regardless of whether or not it was the intended outcome. However, this point in time is an opportunity to look inward as we chart this new path forward. My challenge to you is to push beyond the minimum standards. The inequities in communities require us to think of solutions with a restorative lens. For the communities overburdened by roadway infrastructure, what would improve the lives of the people living there?

In chapter 5, I will go deeper into connecting the engagement process with the technical process. The point of this chapter is to evaluate the baseline policies and practices to allow for better decision-making moving forward.

To get a different outcome, we need a different way of thinking. To address healing the damage done by cars, we need to reframe our thinking from moving vehicles to moving people as well as bring focus to the off-peak times. To address the disparate impacts of historical racism, we need to address the underlying metrics and policies. These are currently barely represented in transportation project planning and implementation. We have work to do.

Moving Cars versus Moving People:
Expand or Redistribute Space

We need to understand and evaluate how space is used within the public right-of-way. Traveling around the United States and crunching data from different cities, you start to see patterns. If a high number of fatalities and serious injuries occur on an urban or suburban roadway, I predict it is probably more than six lanes, people have to travel more than one-half mile to get to a signalized intersection, people driving on the road exceed the speed limit, or all of these. It is the same story in communities across the country.

We are at a pivotal point in history that requires us to do something different. As communities continue to grow, everyone cannot have the expectation of driving in a vehicle by themselves unimpeded during the peak hours. In the same way, retail store parking lots should not be designed for one major shopping week out of the year.

Think about the most congested corridor in your community. What do you see? Is it mostly people in cars by themselves? Do you see any buses or trains? If so, are they full? Do you see people on bicycles, walking, or using a personal mobility device to move around?

Now hold on to that thought. There is the old way to solve the problem by widening the roadway to add more capacity. But we are not doing that.

Another way to evaluate the corridor is by using person throughput as a metric. It provides a framework to redistribute the existing space for solutions that move people. LOS, as I previously discussed, focuses on the volume of vehicles, but person throughput focuses on the volume of people. For example, if you need to move 50,000 vehicles, that is the volume, and either the capacity is available or it does not exist. If the capacity does not exist, your solution is either to widen the road to accommodate the volume or to let people sit in traffic and send angry emails to the mayor. However, if you need to move 50,000 people, you have several options—from each person in their own vehicle to repurposed lanes for public transit to bicycles only (and more). (See figure 3-1.) Moving 50,000 vehicles and moving 50,000 people are not the same thing. The latter would not require widening the road, and, depending on the solution, you may even be able to narrow the roadway, resulting in less maintenance cost—and other benefits.

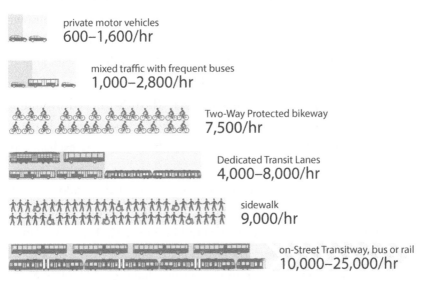

private motor vehicles
600–1,600/hr

mixed traffic with frequent buses
1,000–2,800/hr

Two-Way Protected bikeway
7,500/hr

Dedicated Transit Lanes
4,000–8,000/hr

sidewalk
9,000/hr

on-Street Transitway, bus or rail
10,000–25,000/hr

Figure 3-1: The capacity of a lane based on different modes to illustrate person throughput. (National Association of City Transportation Officials)

For example, I worked on a transit study where the buses made up 3 percent of the volume of vehicles moving through the corridor, but they were moving over 51 percent of the people through that corridor. In other words, the majority of people moving through the corridor were sitting on a bus in traffic caused by the people in cars. We concluded the project with a recommendation to install a bus-only lane and make other improvements so the buses could move faster and allow for more bus service. This meant the majority of people moving through the corridor would be able to move quicker.

At intersections, moving from LOS to person throughput allows for more creative solutions. I worked on one project where the intersection was rated as LOS F. The main reason was that the volume of people using the crosswalk prevented vehicles from being able to turn. People waiting at the traffic signal would have to sit through two or more red lights before they could make a turn. Our team recommended a Barnes Dance, which means people using the crosswalks get their own traffic light cycle, during which they can move in any direction, across or diagonal. With the proposed solution, the number of cars able to drive through the intersection would increase, since they would not have to wait for people to cross the street. The other benefit would be increased safety for people using crosswalks because no vehicle could enter the intersection during the signal phase that was exclusive to people walking.

Going back to thinking about the most congested corridor in your community, what if you could reduce the capacity of that road by two lanes, meaning an eight-lane road would become a six-lane, a six-lane a four, and a four-lane a two? Try not to get distracted by the details; we are just using our imagination to determine what it could look like. Are there more buses on the street now or maybe even a streetcar? Are there bicycle lanes? Are there more trees and landscaping? How has the road changed in your mind from what it is to what it could be?

Another way of redistributing space is examining the networks at a city level to see how the infrastructure is distributed. Do the highways or wide roads affect a specific population? Is there a disproportionate lack of infrastructure for people walking, biking, or riding public transportation in certain areas? Conduct an analysis of the infrastructure versus the community. You should supplement these findings with input from the community. It will give you a clear picture of the population you need to center in your decision-making as you develop alternative solutions. For community advocates and journalists, it will give you the populations that you need to engage and to amplify their voices to get them more resources. In chapter 4, I refer to this group as Silently Suffering.

Finally, for the sake of building an inclusive transportation plan, you will need to center the voices of people who travel during off-peak hours. As an example, schedule data collection during off-peak times. If there are schools, schedule data collection and observations around school arrival and dismissal times and on weekends, when others in the community may be using the playground. I did this for a Safe Routes to School assessment and found that many of the kids were being walked to school by older siblings, who then continued their trip to their own schools. From an engineering standpoint, this means the design requires not only safe routes to the subject school but also safe routes between schools. From a community advocate standpoint, it requires engaging the school of the older sibling, which without engagement might be assumed to fall outside of the project scope.

Another example of land use–specific observations is scheduling data collection around religious institutions. You will want to collect on the day they observe; however, many will also have events during the week such as religious study groups, prayer groups, and community meetings. I had one project where there was an Orthodox synagogue, which means they do not drive when observing the Sabbath and High Holidays. The synagogue provided us with a detailed report noting the paths the congregation walked to get to services.

Reevaluating Metrics: How Are We Measuring Equity?

Building on chapter 2, where we examined what equity looks like: maybe, as in the experience I shared, you came up with a beautifully written statement about what achieving equity means in your city or community. You probably have a clear vision of what it looks like. As with anything in transportation, you have to develop the steps to get there and measure progress along the way. This means reevaluating metrics.

For one mobility project I worked on, the consultant team developed an interim equity report. It has not been released to the public, so I will talk about it in general terms. The purpose of the document was to discuss the existing inequities in a community and create a framework to analyze how the project could meet metrics to address the inequities. The existing condition of a city with its population segregated by race and income is only part of the story. For the interim report, I laid out the story of *how* the city became segregated. This included policies such as redlining, which intentionally kept people out of communities before the civil rights movement, and modern-day displacement in the name of economic development.

Particularly when doing an equity analysis, it is key to examine why the conditions exist as they are. In the equity report, we clearly defined by census tract which communities were bearing the burden of an inequitable transportation system. Therefore, we could measure how the solutions would impact these specific areas. As I mentioned in chapter 2, if you are not specific about who is being harmed, you may continue to cause harm to those communities.

Working with a task force composed of government and nonprofit staff, we asked, "What does equity look like when we achieve it?" The task force members explicitly said that for them, the analysis must show that the commute time would be improved for the areas that the data showed currently had the worse outcomes. This meant looking at the census tracts that had the highest rates of asthma, the longest commute times, and the lowest rates of car ownership. In pushing beyond the bare minimum of analysis, the task force also said the analysis should shorten the commute for residents who had been pushed out of the city by economic development and gentrification.

With the task force's vision as our guidepost, we identified census tracts for further analysis for mobility. After analyzing the displacement of residents over time, we found the census tracts in the neighboring jurisdiction that were the most likely recipients of the displaced residents. Within the city, we found the census tract that had the longest commute times and the lowest rates of car ownership.

None of this would traditionally be looked at in a transportation study, since we do not typically look back. But the importance of these types of analysis is to bring restoration to the community previously harmed.

As you think about a study, plan, or project you may be working on, how can you measure equity? There are two key steps as you reflect. Step 1 is analyzing the history of the community you are studying. Step 2 is working with the community to develop metrics that lead to restoration, which really only that community can articulate.

Step 1: Analyze the History of the Community

Because we are discussing equity and inclusive communities, we need to look at how the inequities were created specifically in that community. I provided two high-level root causes that, in the United States, likely hold true for the area you have in mind. Similarly to the example I provided in this section, you will want to look at the changes over time in that community.

Step 2: Work with the Community to Develop Metrics

Restoration will look different for each community. Remember that the measurement has to tie back into the vision. Some examples are in table 3-1.

Table 3-1: Developing Community Metrics

What Equity Looks Like	Who?*	Example Metrics/Measures
Improved air quality in areas with high childhood asthma rates	Demographic profile of the census tracts with the highest rates of asthma	Reduced number of vehicles driving and idling in the census tracts
		Increased number of street trees planted in the census tracts to improve air quality
Improved commute time for people dependent on public transit	Demographic profile of the census tracts with the longest commutes and lowest car ownership rates	Improved speed for public transit, which may come at the expense of on-street parking and/or general travel lanes
		Improved commute time for residents in those census tracts
Resources prioritized to areas that are on the high injury network and that have historically lacked investment	Demographic profile of communities where there is an overlap of the high injury network and low investment dollars, specifically in relation to investment dollars— highway expansions and interchanges do not count	Short- and long-term investment
		No traffic-related fatalities or serious injuries within those census tracts or areas

* Demographic profile includes race/ethnicity, gender, disabilities, and age. Knowing the "who" will ensure that you are engaging a representative sample of the community. Chapter 5 will go into more detail.

Reevaluating Transportation Policies

Policies lay the foundation for many decisions. For example, I worked with a city that had a policy that the curb-to-curb space could not be expanded unless there were extenuating circumstances, and even then the answer was no. That meant the roadway could not be expanded, but we could do a "road diet," or narrowing of the roadway. As an example, if a road was sixty feet wide from curb to curb, all we had was sixty feet to work with as we developed alternatives to move the growing number of people moving into the corridor. The city's policy decision was "Work with what you have, and if we are going to spend money to reconstruct the road, it will not be to widen it."

Vision Zero could be a path forward as an overall framework for changing policy priorities, but it needs to be more than a plan, and it needs to be crafted with the people. Vision Zero is a concept from Sweden that recognizes we are human and we will make mistakes, but our mistakes should not lead to serious injuries or fatalities. One thing that gets muddled as people in the United States attempt to adopt Vision Zero is conflation of the total number of crashes with the total number of crashes that lead to deaths and serious injuries. Vision Zero does not demand perfect records, and it recognizes that crashes will occur because we are human. Instead, it argues that the focus should be on deaths and serious injuries. The distinction is important because crashes generally happen all over a community and people walk away from fender benders and sideswipes with minor or no injuries. Other than having a bad day, everyone is alive to recount the drama with their family and friends. But the more severe crashes tend to cluster in certain communities. If you focus on crashes regardless of the resulting injury, you may move resources from communities that need them more because they are where people are dying.

The Vision Zero plan of Washington, DC, is a great example of both successful interactions and some shortcomings. In 2015, only a few US cities embraced Vision Zero. DC's plan was one of the first in the United States that included extensive outreach during the plan's development. Over the course of a summer, we had ten meetings on street corners around the city, a youth summit with over two hundred young people, two meetings with special advocacy groups, and meetings with over thirty-five city agencies. We did not just inform people; we also engaged with them and used their feedback and stories to shape the plan. As an example, after talking with a group of young Black teens at the youth summit, we removed all enforcement related to people walking and biking. The young people conveyed to us that sometimes crossing the street midblock got them away from a group of people who may want to cause them harm. The teens weighed their risk of being targeted by violence as higher than their risk of being struck by someone driving a vehicle.

In addition, we heard from people that having police enforce laws related to walking and biking put the community and law enforcement in conflict with each other. Charles T. Brown has documented in his research for his podcast *Arrested Mobility* how laws such as those prohibiting jaywalking are disproportionately enforced[19] in Black and Brown communities, for men in particular. In DC's Vision Zero plan, enforcement was instead targeted to dangerous driving behavior such as excessive speeding, driving under the influence, distracted driving, and reckless driving.

In a world where we are examining policing more closely after George Floyd's murder, I think plans that reexamine equity in this way should take one more step. DC's Vision Zero plan correctly focused on behaviors that lead to deaths and fatalities. However, the plan should have recommended a comprehensive evaluation of *all* the transportation laws and the removal of any that were not supported by data or did not lead to safer streets. If we are discussing data-driven approaches, the laws should target behaviors that lead to crashes that result in deaths and serious injuries.

Moreover, this plan offered recommendations and strategies and did not go further. After the Vision Zero plan was shared, communities were all demanding safer streets. This calls to mind the discussion in chapter 2 of Montgomery County and the tension about who would get resources. All streets could be safer, even if incrementally, and without guiding principles for more of an "emergency room" structure. DC's Vision Zero program led to resources going to where there was advocacy but not necessarily to the areas that needed the investment the most. If you have an opportunity similar to this, I emphasize the importance of putting in a framework that allocates resources to communities and areas experiencing high rates of fatalities and serious injuries, which tend to be the areas with high numbers of Black, Latino, or low-income residents or all of these.

Policy Analysis

Look through some of the policies in your community to see how they may perpetuate inequities. These could include ordinances, city codes, laws, previous plans and studies, or even policy documents—although it is rarely that obvious. Sometimes what may be stated as the policy of a department may actually not be written down, which means it is a practice. If you know, you know, but there is no paper documentation. This could also include policies that you are considering.

Table 3-2 offers ways to evaluate those policies, with examples.

But Should There Be a War on Cars?

No, put down the baseball bats. *But*, to bring together all the elements of this chapter, the more we invest in non-car modes, such as public transportation, bicycles, and pedestrian infrastructure, the more we can bring healing and restoration to communities that were harmed by our predecessors and continue to be harmed by the current infrastructure.

We as a country need to invest more in public transportation. According to the American Public Transportation Association (APTA), public transit is a core strategy to support safe transportation for all people.[20] APTA has documented that 60 percent of public transit users are Black, Latino, or other persons of color; 55 percent are women; and 46 percent live in no-vehicle households.[21] Undergirding this is the fact that using public transportation is safer than driving in a car and allows higher volumes of people to move through a corridor.

Table 3-2: Policy Analysis Guide

Policy	How Could It Harm?	What Would Lead to Restoration?	What Needs to Be Changed to Make This Effective?
Enforcement of jaywalking laws	Community and law enforcement at odds with each other Failure to address why people cross at a particular location (e.g., shortest path to a bus stop, nearest traffic light half a mile away) Responsibility taken away from drivers to avoid hitting someone or something in the roadway Disproportionate enforcement for Black and Brown pedestrians	Removal of the law Evaluation of communities where people are walking midblock for how the crossing could be made safer	The state legislature would need to repeal the law
Statewide mandatory helmet law	Black and Brown men on bicycles disproportionately stopped for not having a helmet	Removal of the law	The state legislature would need to repeal the law
Graduated moving violation and parking fines based on ability to pay	What happens when a person is willing to pay the fine, but it does not change their dangerous driving behavior	City allowed to charge more for people who factor in moving violation and parking fines as a cost of doing business, without financially crushing low-income individuals Opportunity for community service in lieu of payment for people under a certain income threshold	A system would need to be created to determine who falls in which payment category

If you build public transportation, people will give up their cars—if only it were that easy. I will not dive too deeply into a public transportation lesson, but to shift people to transit, it needs to be reliable, have short but predictable wait times between transit vehicles, and take people where they need to go. As I mentioned earlier, reallocating a lane of traffic to be bus only is a great way to move people through a corridor and ensure reliability, since they will not be stuck in traffic.

Biking is another great replacement for driving, especially for trips under three miles. Electronic assist bikes are slowly becoming more affordable, allowing biking to be accessible to more people. Maybe the commute to work is too long for an e-bike, but being able to bike to a park and ride makes transit an option.

In the end, it is not about taking away people's freedom to decide to drive a car. It is about giving people the freedom to use other options to travel to work, play, shop, and whatever else they need to do.

Opportunities for Reflection

We unpacked a lot in this chapter, and I provided you with some activities to evaluate equity. Personal check-in: How are you feeling right now? Confident? Overwhelmed? Did the definition of equity you wrote in chapter 2 change again?

Think about a project; it can be current or past. What are the metrics that would lead to restoration? What would you do differently if you could restart the project today? Would the outcomes change, and if so, how?

CHAPTER 4

Power, Influence, and the Complexity of People

Overall, transportation engineers and planners are not people who shy away from difficulty. Engineering is a hard undergraduate major at any university. It requires several semesters of math and science before you can even take a class within your engineering discipline, and the first two years are filled with challenging classes that weed out all but the most determined students (or the ones who have strong support systems). And then, the majority of transportation planners get a master's degree, an additional two years of writing many papers. However, despite our understanding of differential equations or our graduate-level planning classes, designing a roadway generally comes down to basic math. For example, in allocating space for different modes within a public right-of-way, it often comes down to the width of the public right-of-way as a constraint, and then addition and subtraction to get all the elements within the street to fit.

This is not to oversimplify the design of bike lanes as just a matter of drawing lines on the ground. Frankly, the hardest part is the conflicts at driveways and intersections. But at a conceptual level, most planners and engineers could design bike lanes with relative ease. So why is it so hard to get transportation infrastructure built?

I do not think our education system places enough emphasis on the influence people—supporters, detractors, and the indifferent—can have on a project. And this carries through to how engineers expect to interact with the public in their careers. I have given guest lectures at Cornell University to both high school and college students. As part of the lecture, I gave them a group exercise to design a protected bike lane on a typical street. I gave them the dimensions of the roadway and the minimum requirements for the bike lane. In addition to the design criteria, I provided detailed information about the stakeholders in the corridor. During the group exercise, they were able to ask me clarifying questions. Like true students attracted to science and engineering, they dove right in to solve the problem. Each time I have done this exercise, the groups have been able to provide a conceptual design of a protected bike lane in under ten minutes. I tell them their beautiful designs will never be built because they failed to address the concerns of important stakeholders. Engineering is the "easy" part; multiple stakeholders with differing goals and objectives complicate the project.

Church versus Bikes and the Library Police

While I have plenty of career left, the Eastern Downtown Cycle Track project in Washington, DC, is one of my lower moments. As of this writing, the project is under construction. But it offers myriad examples of how people can make a project difficult—and how different approaches might have made the process less fraught.

For some context, the project area was an approximately 1.6-mile corridor bookended by Howard University to the north and the National Mall to the south, running through some of the densest areas of DC. As with many transportation projects in dense areas, there are diverse and many stakeholders along this corridor. National museums, large entertainment venues such as an arena and theaters, national chain restaurants and retail stores, and office buildings are on the southern end of the corridor. The middle portion of the corridor is a mix of large venues such as a convention center, high- and medium-density apartment buildings, and historically Black churches. At the northern end of the corridor are historic attached homes and small businesses.

Going into the project, the client and the consultant team knew there would be pushback from the churches, based on prior experience with a protected bike lane project that was installed on M Street NW and heavily influenced by parking concerns of a historic Black church.[1] In addition, prior to the Eastern Downtown project, there had been tension between the churches and the community over parking on Sundays.[2] Because of this tension, we started the project by meeting with the churches along the corridor before we made anything about the project public. We listened to their concerns.

At the first public meeting, the plan was to introduce the study and host an open house so people could see the analysis the consultant team had completed to date. Well, that was the plan, anyway. What ended up happening was that the conversations were unproductive and the meeting was over capacity. The library police shut things down halfway into the meeting.

So what went wrong? A great quote from former American baseball player Vernon Law is "Experience is a hard teacher, because she gives the test first, the lesson afterward."

On the surface, you could blame the lack of space in the meeting room or the meeting format. Sure, they were contributing factors. In interviewing my colleagues who worked on the project, I developed a long list of contributing factors. However, the largest misstep going into the project was failure to publicly acknowledge the racial dynamics within the community in the northern half of the project. This is really difficult to do, but it is critically important.

The residential areas of the northern half of the corridor were rapidly changing and gentrifying. Parcels that had been parking lots in 2000 were luxury apartment buildings in 2015, when we were moving forward with our project. What was once the O Street Market, which closed because of crime when the community was majority Black, was now a restored building with a shiny new grocery store and luxury apartments with their own dog park on the roof.[3] The historically Black churches had been witness to all the changes in the neighborhood, starting as early as the 1920s and extending through the riots of 1968, the drug epidemic of the 1980s and 1990s, and revitalization turned gentrification in the early 2000s.

Crime in the 1990s and more affordable large houses in the surrounding DC suburbs drove many Black middle-class residents out of the neighborhood and out of DC. However, on Sundays the former residents returned to their former neighborhood to attend the church that many had grown up in and their families had attended for multiple generations. Lack of adequate public transit on Sunday necessitated driving to church, creating on-street parking challenges. When the neighborhood had vacant parking lots, it was not an issue. But in 2015, the newly developed parcels and new residents in the historic single-family homes reduced the Sunday parking to on-street parking and any off-street parking the church had available. Parishioners started double-parking on the street. New residents were calling parking enforcement on church parishioners. This created a tension between the historically Black churches and new, mostly White residents. And then a bike lane was proposed!

In addition to the racial dynamic between the Black churches and the community, most of the advocates for the protected bike lane were young White people who biked for transportation, whereas most of the church attendees were Black and older. At the first public meeting, well over one hundred people attended. About half were older Black church parishioners, and the other half were young White bike advocates. The Black parishioners showed up early and packed the meeting room, leaving most of the White bike advocates to stand in the back of the room or in the hallway.

It did not help that the local news showed up. Crews filmed the overcrowded hallway with the two groups having tense conversations with each other. Then they interviewed people from both groups, of course picking people with the most dynamic personalities.

In addition to these two racial dynamics, the project team for the consultant and the client were mostly White men. I was the only Black person among the key members of the project team of about ten people. There were three women in total who had regular involvement in the project, many in supporting roles, such as conducting public engagement and assisting with developing the bike lane concepts. During the meeting, the White men in the client and consultant team were in the meeting room with the Black parishioners, while the women on the team were outside in the hallway. It was one of those things no one thought about ahead of time, but the racial contrast between the decision-makers and the community did not go unnoticed.

Beyond the dynamics of race, the other major flaw of the project was that it focused purely on the cycle track. While we should aim to install safe bicycle infrastructure, it was hard to get some community members on board because we were proposing protected bike lanes on streets that did not have sidewalks that were in good condition or wide enough for someone using a wheelchair or pushing a stroller or for two people to walk side by side and have a conversation using American Sign Language, particularly given the number of deaf and hard-of-hearing people attracted to DC by Gallaudet University. Frankly, the whole situation was ableist and lacked any sense of equity. For someone like me, it is easy to walk down a sidewalk even if it is narrow or there are tripping hazards. It is hard to talk about the safety of people biking while ignoring the conditions for people using the sidewalks. When touting the benefit of protected bike lanes for people using the sidewalks, the argument fell flat when the sidewalks were not usable for most people.

The sidewalk was not included because we were attempting to implement the project quickly. The protected bike lane would be in the existing curb line, which would minimize construction to installing a barrier and just require some paint for the bike lane. Adding the sidewalks would require more effort. The street had mature trees, which limited the ability to expand between the existing sidewalk and the curb to make a wider sidewalk. The area between the curb and the property lines included retaining walls, wrought iron fences, trees, gardens, and other obstructions. Even though the retaining walls were within the public right-of-way, it can still be a lengthy process to work with individual property owners. It takes time to convince them their wall is not on their property, and then, once they are convinced, each property must have a design for the new retaining wall or fence. Construction then would require significant coordination with all owners because they would have limited access to the front of their property. Thus, the team rightly anticipated that adding improvements to the sidewalk would increase the cost and duration of the project for both design and construction.

Nonetheless, we should have tackled both from the onset. We easily could have split the project into multiple phases, where the protected bike lane would get installed first, and then the agency would come back and do the sidewalks. We would have needed to have a firm commitment and specific actions to give the community some sense of comfort that we would do the sidewalks in a second phase—but it would have helped with the conversations. (However, if I am being real, the public would not have trusted that the sidewalks would be installed until they were installed.) As with many department of transportation undertakings in which projects are split into multiple phases, sometimes a phase that was promised to the community never gets constructed, and if it does get constructed it is because members of the community continued to advocate for what was promised to them.

Finally, and this was not necessarily a flaw, but we could have done more stakeholder analysis. At the beginning of the project, we did a great job of listing and interviewing key stakeholders. I have probably written hundreds of community stakeholder or public input plans. However, even those lack a critical analysis of the different types of stakeholders. Within the transportation industry, we do not do a great job of knowing the stakeholders beyond the surface level of their interest in the project.

The Project Management Institute has a process to identify stakeholders and analyze their influence and importance as well as assumptions and risks.[4] But even there, a deeper understanding of the stakeholders is missing.

Knowing Your Stakeholders

As my bike lane project amply demonstrated, there are going to be many stakeholders on a project. As you develop your list of stakeholders, you may classify them by land use or social organizations, or if there is an unofficial mayor of the neighborhood, you may even name a specific person. Some key stakeholders may require one-on-one engagement, such as adjacent property owners or schools with complicated drop-off and pick-up operations. We all know, going into a project, that we will never reach 100 percent of the stakeholders in the corridor or study area. Ultimately, the goal of public engagement should be to reach a percentage of the population that represents the total population of that area. Beyond listing the stakeholders, it is important to understand that there are those who hold power and those who are affected (positively and negatively) by the influence of those in power.

Even for advocates and journalists, having an understanding of the key stakeholders allows you to target your messaging and outreach. Who are the people who agree with your position? Who are the people who disagree with you, and why? Is there some core commonality that you can tap into to help them see your side?

Demographic Analysis, or Use Your Eyes

At the beginning of every transportation project, someone on the project will take the lead in drafting the public involvement plan. Generally, the plan should define the goals related to public participation, and then the meat of it will be who, how, and when you will engage the public, including key stakeholders. This will be included in the final report as an appendix, and everyone will get to pat themselves on the back for a job well done.

If there is any federal funding or approvals, the public involvement plan should include a demographic analysis that at a minimum looks at race and ethnicity. If the transportation project will have any federal funding or documents requiring federal approval, it needs to be in compliance with Title VI of the Civil Rights Act of 1964, referred to as Title VI. The law states:

> No person in the United States shall, on the ground of race, color, or national origin, be excluded from participation in, be denied the benefits of, or be subjected to discrimination under any program or activity receiving Federal financial assistance.[5]

The US Department of Transportation has a good tool kit on Title VI and transportation.[6] The tool kit includes fact sheets, guidelines for data collection, and commendable practices. Some state and local governments may have additional requirements, such as for language access and for additional protected classes of people related to gender identity or immigration or housing status. Regardless of the law, the entire purpose of this book is to push beyond the bare minimum for the creation of an inclusive transportation system.

How is Title VI the bare minimum? One of my planning professors called Title VI and the National Environmental Policy Act (NEPA) paper tigers, which outwardly seem powerful but in reality are not as effective as they could be. Essentially, my professor meant that both require documentation and analysis but may not always lead to the best solution. As long as all the boxes are checked and the impacts are considered, it will be difficult to legally challenge the final decision. For example, based on type of environmental document, NEPA outlines what types of meetings are required and when they must be held.

This is the point where I freely admit I have done what I call check-the-box engagement, mainly because public engagement is the first item cut when a project's budget is reduced. If you get nothing else from this chapter, understand that inclusive transportation will require more resources for engagement. And spending resources on engagement might seem trivial, but it can potentially make or break your project.

I consider check-the-box public outreach to be the bare minimum to meet Title VI. This includes having meetings during weekday evenings at a moderately convenient location. The meeting could be advertised in the newspaper, maybe in a flyer sent to the elected representative, and then posted on the agency website and linked to social media. In the end, there is proof of meeting notification, comments are collected at the meeting, a short summary is prepared, and the team is high-fived for a job well done. You have checked the box.

You can show that you attempted to reach all communities, but those who attend the meetings are probably the only ones who are heard in check-the-box engagement. The first step in inclusive transportation is to make sure the engagement process is actually inclusive. This does not mean just inclusively informing people about a meeting. It means taking the extra steps to engage if your meeting outreach does not garner diverse attendance and participation.

Start with a demographic analysis. You will want to map, if possible, race and ethnicity, age, gender, low or no English proficiency, household income, countries of origin, and disabilities. This analysis should be your guide as you move through the project. If the people attending your meetings or engaged in the process do not align roughly with the demographics of the study area, then take a pause to determine how you will proactively reach out to the demographics that are missing. This may require you to adjust the meeting materials, format, location, and time to reach the representative populations. For example, meetings in the evening on a weekday are challenging for people to attend who have small children or who do not work a nine-to-five. I had a project in a neighborhood with a high concentration of older residents where we started meetings at 3:30 p.m. so the older residents could be home before dark in the wintertime.

To have an idea of who still might not be present to offer feedback, you will need to continuously collect and analyze demographic data. This includes tracking the demographics of who is attending your meetings in order to determine who is not attending. Generally, any demographic surveys are optional, so do not overly rely on them. Use your eyes to see who is missing from the engagement, keeping in mind that not all disabilities are visible, not everyone's race or ethnicity is obvious, and some people never seem to age.

People in Power

I developed a working definition of power with my colleagues at the 2018 Salzburg Global Seminar.[7] We defined power as "the ability to direct laws, policies, and investment that shape people's lives."[8] There are levels to power, even if the power is the ability to influence the final decision-maker, who, depending on the community, may be the head of the transportation agency, the city or county manager, or the elected leader (mayor, commissioner, governor). Generally, most transportation projects will not escalate to that level of decision-making. However, every few years there will be one that gets so political that it reaches the desk of an elected leader, grabs the attention of the media, or, in even fewer instances, ends up in the legal system.

In a transportation project, there is the power that you have and the power of the key stakeholders in the process.

Starting with your unique perspective, recognize the power you have over the process. Even if you are not the final decision-maker, you have power within your role in the project. If you are the consultant, you guide the project as it moves through the process and provide advice to your client. If you are the project manager working for a government transportation agency, you are responsible to the day-to-day decisions and briefings to senior leadership. If you are an agency with oversight or approval authority, you determine whether to approve or to require additional analysis. If you are an advocate, you have the power of influence by galvanizing people to attend meetings, submit comments, and email elected officials. If you are a journalist, the way you write about the project can sway public opinion. It is up to you how to use the power you have.

Regardless of who you are, you will want to build the stakeholder list and develop a power analysis. First, develop your list of stakeholders. Then review the list to identify who controls whether or not the change will occur. Who has that authority? Those of you at the transportation agency or consultant company will have the longest list of stakeholders because you will be the one moving the project forward. The head of a transportation agency may have a shorter list of one or two stakeholders, such as the person to convince elected officials that the project should move forward.

The first question—who controls whether or not the change will occur—will help determine who has the power and what type of power they have. It can be tempting to default to the leadership as the ones who control the change and have the most power. However, go through the list to identify others who have control over whether the change occurs. For example, if the project is in a historic district, the state historic preservation officer, local historic review board, or local historic group may have some level of control over the design of the project and how it fits within the study area. Even with an elected leader, look to see whether a big donor is in your study area. Perhaps the power lies in an organization that is a reliable voting bloc that happens to be in the study area.

The second question examines how the individuals have that authority. Elected officials are obvious; they have that authority by the nature of their being elected to represent the people. An unofficial mayor of the neighborhood may have that authority because of their influence in the community. When I lived in Fairfax Village in Southeast DC, an older woman was our unofficial mayor. She influenced whether or not residents attended meetings and whether or not they supported projects. The harder stakeholders to engage are the ones who have invisible and informal authority. For example, they may never attend any public meeting, but they have direct access to a decision-maker such as a big donor to an elected leader, a spouse, a friend, an organization the decision-maker is a member of, or even someone who works for them. Honestly, regardless of how detailed you get with this analysis, you will likely miss the invisible people because they like being the power brokers in the shadows. But you may encounter them as the project moves forward, and you should be prepared to add them to the list of people who may need one-on-one contact.

Once you identify the people in power, it is important to ask: What do they care about? What do they value? What may be their concerns about the project? What do they need to see to support the project?

For people who hold power, you will need to determine the right time to engage them in the process. For elected officials and leaders of a transportation agency, you will want to engage them in the project before you do anything that goes out to the public, especially if you know the project has the potential to be high profile or controversial. Nothing is worse than having a leader caught off guard because they did not know you were doing the project. If you can, provide them with an opportunity to speak candidly and off the record. With the Freedom of Information Act (FOIA) this can be tricky, because your notes and any recordings you make could be part of the public record even if you are a consultant. My recommendation is to take notes on their concerns and ideas but do not attribute the comment to them unless you get their permission.

For others with power, you may take a blended approach when you speak with them. With some, such as unofficial mayors and leaders of advocacy organizations, you may want to have an informal or formal conversation early in the project. With others, you may want to wait until you are further along in the process and maybe have the support of people who can influence their support of the project.

The group I call People in Power is probably the most complicated group you will work with, and it requires political savvy to identify the people and organizations that have power. You will need someone on your team who is entrenched in the community and can guide you in this area. However, a big word of warning: do not use that person's political capital and then not include them in a key role in the project. People who are entrenched in the community have put in the time to build trust with that community. Regardless, if you are the government, consultant, advocate, or journalist, do not use this person for their Rolodex.

Naysayers

Sometimes the planning world will refer to the group I call Naysayers as NIMBYs. The term "NIMBY" (not in my backyard) started in the

1970s, when communities were pushing back against harmful land uses such as landfills, highways, and nuclear power plants.[9] In today's transportation world, NIMBYs generally oppose anything that changes the status quo. They may support protected bike lanes, but one street over and not on their specific block.

Needless to say, the Naysayers can sometimes be more complicated than people who simply say no to everything. Yes, there are groups of people who will say no to any changes to their community because they are perfectly content with the status quo. Even in the middle of a dense urban area, with neighbors who have diverse needs, they will balk at anything that changes their peaceful existence. There are also Naysayers who do not want a project because of the negative impacts to their community, such as a highway expansion that will require people to relocate. It can be tempting to dismiss the Naysayers' concerns as trivial, selfish, or worse, nonsensical. As we try to make better transportation decisions for the future, including creating equitable and inclusive transportation networks, some projects will still create what are perceived as negative impacts. Adding a sidewalk may result in loss of on-street parking, which may concern a Naysayer. If Naysayers are trying to avoid negative impacts to their community, their feelings are valid.

Do not ignore the Naysayers. Engaging this group of stakeholders will sometimes require the ability to ask the right questions to get to their real concerns. You will have to listen closely to their concerns and determine what is perhaps a far-fetched concern, what is a red herring, and what has real implications and would cause negative impacts if the project moves forward. For example, in the case study I referred to at the beginning of the chapter, the Naysayers, in that case the historical Black churches, stated loss of parking, traffic, and safety as their reasons for not wanting the bike lanes. However, even when provided with data to the contrary, they held to that position. At the root of the root was a community grasping its identity as it was rapidly gentrifying. The parishioners feared having to relocate their church, just as other historical Black churches that felt the strains of gentrification had relocated to Prince George's County in Maryland.[10]

I had one project where three older Black women did not want protected bike lanes. When I asked why, they stated loss of parking as the reason. However, I continued to probe by asking "why" questions. After about ten minutes, they confessed they did not want the bike lanes because they did not know how to bike. By the end of the meeting, they were still skeptical, but they were more open to the idea of protected bike lanes.

If you do enough projects in an area, you will know who some of the Naysayers are before a project even starts. Some of them will have reputations in the community for being vocal at meetings and opposed to any changes. These stakeholders will be easy to identify. For some other Naysayers, you will need additional analysis.

Start by asking, Who benefits from the existing condition? The Naysayers are perfectly satisfied by the status quo. Maybe they can park their car directly in front of their house for free, or maybe they can control who can and cannot live on their block, or maybe they do not want their community destroyed by an expanded roadway or a highway that bypasses them altogether. Understanding who benefits from the existing conditions could reveal who may be the most resistant to change.

As you analyze this group, be as specific as possible. How do they benefit from the existing condition? What would they have to give up for things to change? What will happen to them if things change?

Champions

The Champions are the ones who want something different. They are vocal advocates demanding change, and often they are the reason the project is even happening. They may be organized and able to galvanize people to attend meetings, sign petitions, or write to their elected officials.

Who wants something different? Why do they want change? What is the outcome they desire? The last question is important. It will take practice, but you will have to discern what they mean and roll this up into a big picture outcome. For example, on a protected bike lane project, it can be tempting to be specific and say this group champions a protected bike lane on a specific street. However, the big picture desired outcome may be that they want a protected north–south route.

In the case of building a highway, the group may support the proposed highway, but ultimately what they really want is not to have to sit in congestion on their commute. Having the big picture view of their outcome gives you the space to give them what they desire in another way. Instead of an expanded highway, perhaps high-occupancy vehicle (HOV) or managed lanes could be installed within the general-purpose lanes.

Everyone loves people who enthusiastically support a project. However, keep in mind two cautions with your Champions. First, the Champions' enthusiasm can actually work against the project. For example, in the case study at the beginning of the chapter, the bicycle advocacy organization did a great job of getting people to the meeting; however, the people at the meeting lacked diversity and true representation of the people who lived and biked in the corridor. This fed the underlying tensions in the community. Second, the Champions can hold you to a project that you cannot implement. As you are balancing feedback from the public, it eventually must translate into design. There may be compromises along the way. Some Champions will understand, but others may transition to Naysayers if they feel the design is too compromised.

Silently Suffering

As I mentioned in chapter 2, the Silently Suffering group is where the test of equity will happen. How the project sponsor addresses or does not address this group will show quickly whether equity is a buzzword of the organization or an ingrained practice. Engaging this group requires going beyond check-the-box public engagement.

Regarding the needs of the project, often the Silently Suffering will be the group you need to center throughout the process. That is, when it comes to decision points, this is the group whose needs should be prioritized. Yes, prioritized. That may not feel inclusive, but engineers, planners, and elected leaders have to make hard decisions. For example, let's say you are trying to install a sidewalk so children can walk to school safely, but the stakeholders in the community are split between Champions and Naysayers. At some point, you may have to decide. If you are centering the Silently Suffering, the children's need to walk to school safely should be the priority.

As you develop your public involvement plan, target and center the Silently Suffering. Recognize whose voice is not being heard in the process, and then be proactive and reach out to those communities. Champions and Naysayers may also suffer, but go deeper to root out the Silently Suffering. Usually, they will not be engaged in the process because they are intentionally or unintentionally excluded from the process. As an example, if you are analyzing bus service, the people who rely on the bus the most may use it during off-peak hours, including late at night. Yet meetings about the bus route may be held in a location that is inaccessible by bus or at a time when people who are most dependent on the bus are not able to attend.

A really important note for advocates working with the Silently Suffering is to amplify the voices of this group. It can be tempting to speak for them, which can sometimes lead to speaking over them. The name Silently Suffering does not imply that you need to save them. As you engage, check your motivations. Are you engaging them because they are a means to your end? Part of engagement is to reach out to them and allow them to use your platform to describe how the project would benefit or harm them.

For the Silently Suffering, who is hurt by the existing condition, or who could be hurt if you make a change without their input? They are constantly harmed by decisions (and indecision, which is also a decision). The data show that these are consistently the ones killed or seriously injured in traffic crashes, the ones with unreliable bus service, the ones living with poor air quality from traffic congestion.

Final Note about Public Engagement

I would be remiss if I did not provide fair warning that public engagement can be challenging. Every city has areas that will always be challenging because everyone living there is an armchair urban planner or engineer. It will be hard not to take the yelling personally, but know that it is not you they are yelling at.

However, public engagement can be rewarding. Codesigning with the community can improve your skills as you learn from each community. For example, I worked on a transit project aimed at people with disabilities and older adults. Other than needing glasses to see far, I do not have any disabilities that prevent me from moving around. Working on the project brought my awareness of people with disabilities to another level. I learned to consider all types of needs, from designing a public meeting to accommodate multiple disabilities to planning a meeting to coincide with days disabled or older people can travel for free or reduced rates using taxis. I adopted a new presentation style in which I did not rely on people's ability to see a PowerPoint slide and made sure to use the microphone to ensure people's hearing aids could pick up a consistent volume. Even public meetings interrupted by the library police are opportunities to learn.

Opportunity for Reflection: Framework

Note for people working in government: this exercise may be subject to FOIA request, so be mindful of the medium in which you share this information. You may need to rename the groups to something that does not make the cover of your local newspaper. But I am trying to be very clear, not political, in table 4-1.

Table 4-1: Understanding People

People in Power	What do they care about?
	What do they value?
	What may be their concerns about the project?
	What do they need to see to support the project?
Naysayers	Who benefits from the existing condition?
	How do they benefit from the existing condition?
	What would they have to give up for things to change?
	What will happen to them if things change?
Champions	Who wants something different?
	Why do they want change?
	What is the outcome they desire?
Silently Suffering	Who is being hurt by the existing condition?
	Who could be hurt if you make a change without their input?

Note: This builds on the "Confronting Power and Privilege for Inclusive, Equitable and Healthy Communities" framework that Veronica O. Davis coauthored at the Salzburg Global Seminar. It fits the framework to the groups the author has laid out in the chapter.

CHAPTER 5

Bringing People and Planning Together

IN THE TRANSPORTATION INDUSTRY, especially as people overuse the word "equity," we recognize the need to engage the public and stakeholders. I have seen (and probably have created) process graphics that show how the community will be engaged throughout the planning process. Consultants' two favorite phrases for public engagement are "early and often" and "continuously engaging throughout the process." However, without fail, the planning process and public engagement process run parallel but do not do a good job of informing each other. By this, I mean there is a technical process focused on the elements that impact the conceptual design or the alternatives, and there is a public engagement process to get feedback, but it is not often clear how the public feedback shapes the final alternative.

Frankly, sometimes the disconnect is intentional. There will be an elaborate and creative engagement process, the feedback will be summarized to prepare an outreach summary or meet the requirements of Title VI of the Civil Rights Act of 1964, but ultimately the agency has an objective and will continue to march toward that objective. At other times, the public engagement process is genuine, but the Naysayers are the loudest voice at public meetings or the People in Power do not fully support the process, so the politics and the optics tend to drive the entire decision process.

Have you witnessed this type of disconnect in your transportation projects? If you happen to be an advocate reading this, do you get frustrated because it seems like the comments you provide fall into an abyss? Do you get fatigued from providing input while nothing seems to change?

Why Is There a Disconnect?

In my experience, there are four big reasons why there is a disconnect between the planning process and the public engagement process. (There are probably more.)

1. The engagement team is not included in the technical process.
2. The transportation team knows what it wants to do.
3. Planners and engineers are not trained in effective public engagement.
4. Governments are sometimes afraid of the public.

As you read the expanded discussions of these reasons, I hope that if some words strike you as something you may have experienced on a project, you will take time to reflect. Why was the process disconnected? What would you do differently if you could do the project again?

The Engagement Team Is Not Included in the Technical Process

I mentioned this in previous chapters, but it bears repeating because the engagement team is so often excluded. Changing this is one of the principal ways we can center people in transportation decisions. Usually, the person or consulting firm leading engagement is not involved in the technical process. Generally, the prime consultant will bring on an outreach firm as a small business partner. It is one of the easiest parts of the project to subcontract to meet the women, minority, and disadvantaged enterprise percentages. Most outreach firms specialize in communications, marketing, meeting logistics, grassroots engagement, or all of these. Some small firms do both technical work and engagement but are assigned only to the engagement team.

Regardless of what the request for proposal says about the need for "robust" or "comprehensive" public engagement, in any project one of the first items cut during cost negotiations is either public engagement or time allotted for project management, which includes team meetings. To save the budget, the person leading public engagement is excluded from the project management and technical team meetings but is still expected to put together a public meeting to get feedback.

The disconnect is compounded because project managers often do not understand engagement, or it is not something that is a strength for them. Very few project managers have both strength in the technical components and ideas for how to engage the public. A public engagement lead who is not included in technical meetings is left to rely on the project manager to communicate guidance from the client in the public engagement process. We have all played "telephone" and understand how this puts clear communication at risk.

Additionally, a public engagement lead who is not part of the technical process is essentially planning meetings without knowing what type of feedback will be useful for the technical process. This can backfire by making the public feel their concerns are being ignored—and result in genuine missed opportunities to make the project serve the community better. An example is creating a public meeting that has engaging activities but does not result in feedback that is truly useful to the technical process.

The Transportation Team Knows What It Wants to Do

This is probably the hardest for government agencies and consultants to admit. Before community members and advocates go "Aha! I knew it," understand that this is not always the case. However, in some projects, the city, county, or state government already knows what it wants to implement, and the team has to create a pretend process to get the public to draw the same conclusion. I know, this is probably the most shocking thing I have written. However, it happens. But before you go shaking your fist at some poor engineer who works for the city or its consultants, recall the stakeholder group People in Power (see chapter 4). That engineer or planner works for the city, and the city's consultants are doing their best to deliver a project, as well as ensure they stay employed. Sometimes they toe the party line and parrot whatever the powers that be have said. Sometimes they disagree but use the opportunity to make the best of the situation.

Most of the time, the public can see this for what it is and will even publicly state that the government entity already knows what it wants to do. Savvy members of the public will submit Freedom of Information Act (FOIA) requests to get the documents or other information about the project.

It is not necessarily a bad thing that a government agency has an idea of what it wants to implement. Particularly when it comes to safety, there may be nonnegotiables, so public input will not change the project. If that is the case, the best thing to do is to be up-front with the public about what you are trying to achieve, why you are trying to achieve that goal, and what type of input you want from them.

For example, if you are trying to design and construct a sidewalk to provide a place for children to walk, bike, or use a wheelchair to get to school, the public involvement process will be less focused on engagement and more informational. Members of the public may not want the sidewalk, but from a safety perspective (or in cities where laws require sidewalks), the project is nonnegotiable.

Planners and Engineers Are Not Trained in Effective Public Engagement

Another reason these processes might not synchronize is that engineers and even some planners are not taught how to interact with the community. Some planning schools may have a community development class in which students, with guidance, work on a project with a community. But the students are not taught how to structure a meeting, how to interact with the public, or, most important, how to incorporate that public feedback into the planning process. More emphasis on this aspect of the job is needed in courses because it rarely comes naturally to people drawn to engineering fields. And it is a skill that can be cultivated, not necessarily something you are born knowing how to do.

In my five years of studying civil engineering in undergraduate and graduate school, I did not have a single course or even lecture that discussed public outreach. Even though I had to take two English classes for my undergraduate degree, I never learned how to communicate with the public while in school. For my planning degree, I learned how to create maps, but I never learned how to create visuals to help the public understand the purpose of a project and what is being proposed.

Fortunately, this is slowly changing. Universities are doing more engagement with the transportation industry to know how to shape the curriculum so students will be better prepared for the workforce. This includes more conversations about public engagement. But as conversations become more fraught and, frankly, political, educators need to make sure their graduates are prepared for potentially difficult situations. Continued attacks on critical race theory and equity in higher education curricula create uncertainty for some professors without tenure. What can they teach within the ever-changing rules?

Governments Are Sometimes Afraid of the Public

Finally, my personal favorite reason for dysfunction in transportation projects is that governments are sometimes afraid of the public. I have worked with governments up and down the East Coast, and there are some planners and engineers who fear the public. It is actually an interesting cycle to watch. The government entity did not listen to the community in the past, so every time it shows up for new community feedback, the community gets upset and brings up the issue from the past. The engineers or planners do not want to be yelled at by the public, so they create a process to minimize public engagement or concoct a convoluted faux-engagement process really designed to avoid getting yelled at. Then the community gets upset and sends emails or posts comments on the internet, which leads to engineers and planners being scared of the community. Rinse and repeat.

As an example, I had a project in a community that was very engaged and generally challenging for accomplishing projects. But in this case, they were generally supportive of the project, aside from some specific concerns about trees, which I communicated to the project team at the beginning of the project.

The engineers responsible for design and construction did not want to do public engagement because it was a vocal community. We ended up doing one open house meeting, with the engineering team avoiding talking to the community. Community members got upset because the engineers were not listening to them. These were not Naysayers doing everything in their power to torpedo the project. They had concerns that were relatively minor, related to trees. I had recommended to the project manager to promise to have a tree committee when it got to that part of the project—simple and inexpensive. But the engineering team did not want to engage because the community had been difficult on other projects. In the end, the project was shelved because of "community controversy."

Challenges with Current Analysis Methods

How to avoid some of these pitfalls? Be aware of history. History need not always go back to the founding of the community; sometimes it goes only as far back as the last promise to the community, which may have been within the past year. I have been in meetings where community members brought letters and emails, or name-dropped previous leaders who made a promise years ago and the community was still waiting on that promise. Not taking the time to understand the history of a place will leave you with a derailed community meeting and public engagement process. Think about it from the community's perspective. You are asking for their input on a project when you failed to deliver on a previous promise. And it does not matter if it was literally you or not.

Governments forget because of staff attrition, but people in communities do not forget. Long-term residents have long memories, and new residents get the stories from the long-term residents. As part of documenting the existing conditions, interview residents who have been in the community for a while. They will be great sources of information about the history. Often, the existing condition includes how they remember the roadway of their younger days. It is like how my mom still can recall details of growing up before the state constructed the highway. And valuing this more will lead to focusing on how to bring together the project's planning and design elements and the public engagement elements.

Linking Planning and Design with Public Engagement

I have tried to clearly emphasize that to be effective, the planning and design process and the public engagement process must go together. At the foundation, this requires governments to ensure there is adequate funding for public engagement, including provision of supportive services such as online engagement, babysitting, transportation, or a meal so people can participate in the public meeting. Procurement rules can be a barrier, but if you are able, try to pay people and organizations for their time and their ideas. But assuming all foundations exist, how can the processes go together?

Generally, any project starts with data collection, which informs the existing conditions. Once the existing conditions are known, the team develops alternatives. This can be done in several ways. Sometimes every possible alternative is identified and then a screening process is undertaken to reduce these to three to five via an alternatives analysis. Depending on the size of the project, a recommended alternative may move into design or an environmental process may identify the preferred alternative, which then moves into design. The more complicated the project, the more engagement and analysis are needed. Regardless, the high-level process is still generally the same.

So the questions become when to engage the public and how to use their input throughout the project. The "when" may be dictated by a regulatory process, so make sure to identify any mandated engagement timelines. For example, any project for which an environmental impact statement is required under the National Environmental Policy Act (NEPA) has very specific touchpoints with the public and specific notice criteria. Agencies can and should go above and beyond, but make sure any engagement process includes what is legally required. If there is a lawsuit, which is very common with environmental impact statements, if you missed any mandated public outreach, you did not follow the NEPA process.

I said it earlier, but it bears repeating. NEPA is a paper tiger. It is very hard to sue on what the agency decided as a preferred alternative. It is very easy to sue on the process to get to that decision, and public engagement is part of that process.

The "how" to use the public's input requires time spent in reframing input from the public engagement into qualitative data. Generally, with the old way of thinking regarding public feedback, you would collect data, summarize the meeting, and move on. However, if you treat public input as qualitative data, it may change how you need to collect feedback and how best to analyze it. What follows is some guidance for making the raw feedback from the public into something useful.

Data Collection

No matter what the project is, you will need to collect data to start the project. That may mean going to the project location and physically collecting the data, or it may mean pulling information from previous studies and reports. Either way, at the beginning of the project, there will be a list of data you will need in order to prepare the existing conditions report. Included in that data should be the lived experience of the community. Yes, the lived experience of the community constitutes data.

How do you get information from the public if you have not yet held a public meeting? Even in Silently Suffering communities, data are available. The community has already told you the problem. The data include, but are not limited to, service requests submitted through 311 or a comparable system, emails to government and elected officials' staffs, comments on previous studies, and comments posted on social media, including blogs. Also reach out to other agencies to see if they have any information from the public in the study area.

This can be a resource-intensive exercise, but it is a great job for an intern or a junior staff member. It is worth having the background information to provide a sense of the neighborhood issues and ideas. It will also give you information about land mines to avoid.

Another important reason for this step is that at the first public meeting, you will want to start the conversation with what you have already heard from the community over the years. If you do not address concerns that community members have already stated, they will start the process agitated.

GET STAFF TO SPILL THE BEANS

Large organizations, which include governments, are siloed. But it is important to remember that to the public, the government is simply the government. There may be another agency doing a non-transportation project in the community that they are upset about. You do not want that to derail your project, but it certainly could if you are not prepared—because you are all "government."

Have a kickoff meeting with all groups within the transportation and planning agencies that have projects in the planning or study area. If there are other government entities in the study area, such as libraries or schools, you may want to reach out to them as well.

What work have they already done in the neighborhood? This can include any data they may have, previous studies and plans, and contact information for leaders in the community.

What have they heard from the public? Whenever the public has an audience with staff from the government, they will bring up all the issues they have in their neighborhood, even if these are outside the purview of the staff. You will want to know what they have heard from the public. What are their concerns and their ideas?

What promises have been made to the public? This is an important question. Government staff may have made a promise to the community.

However, it may not be documented anywhere, and the person who made the promise may no longer be in that position. You will want to know what has been promised. You do not necessarily need to honor the promise, especially if it was made a long time ago or standards have changed since then. If you are not going to honor the promise, you will need to thoroughly document and explain why. You cannot just ignore it.

For example, let's say someone promised to never install a sidewalk. However, the law changed and now requires sidewalks on both sides of the street. In this case, you may not be able to honor that promise, but you don't want to have a surprise antagonistic conversation with people who feel betrayed.

What are small outstanding issues that can be addressed before the project starts? If the community has been complaining about something small, like the need to repaint a crosswalk or replace a sign, you will want to know. If at all possible, to try get those items addressed before the first public meeting. The engagement process can be derailed if such issues are not addressed or there is not at least a timeline to address them.

Get the Elected Officials to Talk

Elected officials are People in Power, regardless of the management structure. They were voted into their position by the public, and therefore they represent their constituents. When constituents get upset, they email their elected officials to complain. Every now and then, when the Champions mobilize people, they will get emails from constituents who support the project. All this is to say you will really want to engage elected officials at the beginning of the project and at key points throughout.

This will depend on the rules of engagement where the project is occurring, but try to brief all elected officials within or immediately adjacent to the project area. In some cases, the project manager or the consultant may be able to do the briefing. In some places, the director or a government relations person will be required to engage the elected officials.

Make sure you know the sunshine laws of the area so that you know what is an official versus an unofficial meeting with an elected official. For example, in some places, the presence of more than two council members in the meeting constitutes a public meeting, which requires public notice and documentation. How much or how little the elected official talks will depend on their comfort level. If the meeting is off the record, you may get more information, but you will have to be very careful how that information is shared so it does not become part of a FOIA request.

In addition to, or in lieu of, meeting with the official, you may want to meet with their staff. Often, the staff members are the ones who respond to calls and emails from constituents. They sometimes have a better pulse on the community than the elected official.

Whether it is the elected official, their staff, or both, brief them on the project, what you intend to accomplish, and the overall timeline. Ask them if they have any concerns or ideas about the project. Before you leave, ask whether they have contact information for any key stakeholders and groups that need to be engaged in the process. The list they provide will give you a sense of who influences the elected official.

Foundation for the Project

All the information you have collected is your starting point for the project. You have at least an idea of the issues and ideas from the public. For information that can be displayed spatially, I recommend inputting the information into a map. Other options are summarizing the information and pulling out the big themes and ideas. The data from the public are just as important as the technical data that you collect. These data begin to create a story. Also, they will give you a sense of where the land mines are and how to strategically navigate around them.

Over my professional career, I have reviewed and written countless existing conditions reports. You probably have too. They are so common because we are hoping to achieve a baseline understanding of the need for and purpose of the project. But a significant shortcoming with existing conditions analyses for transportation projects is that they focus on the physical infrastructure, such as the street itself, sidewalks, bus stops, trees, and, every so often, land use. The existing conditions are more than the physical conditions. They are also about the people who are using or cannot use the transportation system. We need to focus more on what transportation does for people—both harm and benefit—than an existing conditions analysis is designed to evaluate.

For projects that will have to go through NEPA, try to use the public comments as part of the need for the project. For NEPA, defining the purpose and need will set the framework for how the alternatives are created and evaluated. Do they meet the purpose and need? The exact process may vary from state to state. However, in general, the purpose and need statement should be shaped by data that identify why the project is being carried out.

As an example, safety could be a need of the project, backed up by data related to crashes resulting in serious injuries and fatalities. Information from the public can be included in the purpose and need statement as a qualitative data point that brings a story to the quantitative data.

Beyond any comments provided by the public on the physical infrastructure, see if they have provided comments about meeting times, days of the week, or locations. For example, I have seen comments from previous meetings that remind the project sponsor not to schedule meetings during religious holidays or to avoid meeting locations that require government-issued identification to enter.

First Interactions with the Public for the Project

Now you are ready for your first public interaction for the project. A word of warning: do not start with "Tell me all your problems"—it will not go well, for two main reasons. One, as I mentioned earlier, this sets up the public to be frustrated because they have already provided input, even if that input was a decade ago. The public will expect that the information has been shared. Two, to avoid frustration later in the project, provide some context and framework for the type of information you want from the public. It is not necessarily about taking potential alternatives off the table from the beginning, but you do not want to set up unrealistic expectations. As with my example earlier—if there are laws against widening a sidewalk, say so.

As an example, I worked on a transit planning study to examine where the buses were bunching on the street and provide recommendations to improve reliability. The consultant team prepared a detailed existing conditions report that included data from riding the buses during different times of the day, transit agency data such as from automatic vehicle locators and automatic passenger counters, and a physical assessment of bus stop access. Going into the first public meeting, we had a good understanding of where the buses were getting off schedule.

At the first public meeting, we shared what we had heard from the public prior to the study and the technical observations. Instead of asking the community where the buses were having problems, we had a community mapping exercise asking community members why the buses were getting off schedule in certain areas. For example, one bus stop had a high number of people getting on, despite the fact that the land use around the stop would not seem to support the volume of ridership. In talking with the community, we learned that areas of the neighborhood did not have residential parking, so people were driving in from other places, parking in the neighborhood, and then getting on the bus. The neighborhood was serving as an informal park and ride. Similarly, we learned that another stop was an informal kiss and ride, where people were getting dropped off by someone else. I am not sure we would have learned that information on our own because we were focused on the bus route and the ridership data. Probably not.

You will want to distill all the information you collect and present it back to the public in a way that is tangible. If there is a presentation, it can be included in a few slides. If there are boards or handouts, it could be summarized there. You will want to clearly and concisely acknowledge that you have heard the community members. You can start by saying, "This is what we heard from you and how we heard it; did we miss anything?" This enables the community members who were engaged in previous processes to feel heard and concur with what you have heard. The question "Did we miss anything?" gives the public an opportunity to add any new concerns or, for new members of the community, an opportunity to feel heard.

Community Input

For the purposes of this chapter, which focuses on better ways to connect the planning and design and the public engagement parts of the project, I recommend two ways to use community input to determine the existing conditions. One, to get the history, and two, to unpack more of the "why."

Community members can be very valuable in unpacking the history, if you dare or care to ask, particularly in communities that existed prior to the automobile or that were designed for walking. Taking the time to talk with older residents will give you perspective on the community. They will often name people who lived in the community. For example, my mom still remembers what life was like before the highway or wide road divided their community. This knowledge will be valuable to you if you want to figure out how your work might help restore some of the community fabric that has been lost, or how to provide services or access that were taken from them by previous infrastructure. That should be the kind of grade A we are looking for.

The residents may be able to provide historical photos of the community or the name of the community historian. On one of my projects, a taxi driver who was a long-term resident provided historical context, including the title of a book at the library containing a treasure trove of photos that showed the neighborhood prior to urban renewal in the 1960s.

The other side of community input is getting information about why things are happening. One way to get this input is by community mapping, which can be done digitally, using an application, or on good old-fashioned paper. Community mapping literally is having a map on which people can add comments spatially. For example, if you are trying to provide safe routes to school, you may have parents draw on a map where they observe people speeding or where most children cross the street. As you interact with the community, you will have to ask probing questions to get an understanding of why a problem is happening. It will help to engage the public and note their comments spatially. In the next case study, toward the end of the chapter, I will explore this in more depth.

The Process

A little secret. Regardless of how many projects happen in an area, the public does not understand the process. There may be urban planners or engineers who live in the community and will try to explain the process to their neighbors. Or there could be armchair planners or engineers who have some understanding of the process. They will range from being able to accurately describe the process to providing misinformation, but because they can talk the talk, they will be seen by their neighbors as an authority on the subject. It can be very helpful to understand who these people are to make sure you aren't also playing a game of telephone, courtesy of them.

At the first public meeting, it is so important to lay out the process to make sure everyone is truly on the same page. A diagram is useful to graphically explain what is going to happen. However, I recommend being more detailed by providing the following information.

What is going to happen when. This sets the expectation for the public process. It tells the community when they can expect to have another meeting or interaction, what information will be shared by the project team, and the type of feedback they will be expected to provide. For example:

At the second public meeting, we will provide an overview of our assessment of the challenges and opportunities in the corridor based on data we collected and input from the public at this meeting, share how we will create potential solutions in the next phase, and display all the alternatives we will evaluate. We will release the summary report to the public thirty days before the meeting. We will ask the public to provide final feedback on the report to confirm we did not miss anything and identify any other alternatives we should consider for the first evaluation. You will be able to provide feedback online, via mail-in form, at the meeting, or by calling XXX-XXX-XXXX. We expect the meeting to be in October.

In the example, the community knows what information to expect at the next meeting. They are provided with a general time frame for the meeting. In addition, they are given information about when any documents will be released.

Who is making the decision. This is a tough one because it can be hard to get someone to own the decision. This is especially true when the project may be controversial. Depending on the nature of the project, the decision-maker could be a project manager for the agency or a department head. But being coy with the public rarely goes well. Be clear about who is making the decision, whether it is the project manager, the project team, the director, or an elected official. If you are not clear about who is the decision-maker, the public will often go to the highest-ranking person, who is usually the highest elected official.

What information the project team will use to make the decision. You do not have to go into specifics, but it is helpful to share the decision-making process. It can be as simple as a decision matrix or a framework. How you evaluate the decision should tie directly into why this project is happening in the first place.

Subsequent Meetings

After each meeting, if you collect any public comments, they should be summarized in a public meeting summary. At a minimum, this should include details about the meeting, such as when and where the meeting was held, how many people attended, and the big themes you heard from the public. Since we are pushing beyond the minimum, I recommend it also include a demographic summary of who attended compared with the demographics of the community, unedited comments from the public, and how the public comments will be used in the next phase of the project. The summary should be shared with the public within two to three weeks of the meeting. For meetings with larger attendance, you may need more time to summarize the comments.

At subsequent meetings, you should give a summary stating "This is what we heard" during the previous phase and outline how you addressed the comments and why. This can be shared in the presentation, on a display board, on the meeting handout, or all three. As you move through the project, it has to be clear to the public how you are using their feedback to move from one phase to the next.

At the End—Respond

At some point, the project will come to an end, and there will be a final report with recommendations. There are a couple of options for addressing final comments.

Option one is to address them in the final report. At a minimum, the public engagement section of the final report should outline when, where, and how the public was engaged. It should also include any demographic information in comparison with the community as a whole. Then, either in the public engagement section or throughout the analysis section, there should be a summary of public comments throughout the process and how they were used to shape the decision. This is also a good opportunity to acknowledge any outstanding items from the public comments that should be addressed in the design or operations process of the project.

The final report is a technical document, but it should also tell a story that provides context for how the project team arrived at the final decision. The individual summaries for each outreach event can be included in an appendix. The key is to be transparent regarding the decisions made and how the public comments helped in making those decisions.

Option two is to address the public in a "response to comments" document. Take all the comments in the final report and place them in a spreadsheet. One by one, respond to them. Some responses may just be "Thank you for your feedback." For comments that ask questions regarding anything in the final report, respond to the question as completely as possible.

Transparency Can Be Scary

Everything in this chapter works only if the project sponsor is willing to be transparent with the public. I acknowledge that transparency can be scary even when the project sponsor has all the best intentions. Once information is released to the public, it can be misinterpreted. It also becomes hard to hide a mistake. However, as I mentioned earlier, you can proactively share information with the public and build trust, or you can keep the information close and have the public submit a FOIA request after the fact.

Personally, I recommend avoiding having the public submit a records request to get information. Once you have provided information or data via a FOIA request, you have lost the ability to provide context and craft your story. It is all handed to the requester and left to them to craft the story, which often will not work in your favor. The best way to avoid this is by preparing the information yourself in a one-page summary, a report, or even a blog post that can provide context for the data people are reviewing. Post the information on the project's website. It's much better to address it in your own report. People may still request your emails and other documentation, but usually if they are reviewing emails they are grasping at straws and looking for a gotcha.

Example: Bringing It All Together

I was the project manager for a livability study. My goal was to make sure the public engagement process would meaningfully inform the design and planning elements that would follow. Within portions of the study areas, there were recently completed safety studies. In addition, other transportation-related studies had been completed within the past decade in the study areas. And there were areas of the community with very vocal constituencies. Needless to say, there were plenty of public comments in the area.

As with most other transportation projects, we went through all the previous studies and pulled out the recommendations. We created a master spreadsheet and used the recommendations as a starting point.

Next, we went through all available public data including, but not limited to, 311 requests, safety requests, and emails. We also got lucky in that we had data on the public's perceptions of unsafe conditions that had been collected as part of the Vision Zero Action Plan project.

We had an interagency kickoff meeting that included different groups within the transportation department, the planning department, the environmental department, and the water and wastewater utility. In this meeting, we collected what they had heard from the public, any promises they had made to the public, and any ideas they wanted us to consider.

Finally, we conducted an internet search for any comments related to transportation in the study areas. This included social media, blogs, local newsletters, and meeting minutes from civic organizations.

We compiled all this information in a master spreadsheet that we called "All the possible ideas." We noted the sources of the information. We then went through the spreadsheet to identify anything that was a maintenance request that could be completed quickly and anything that was outside the scope of the project. We then created a new sheet with just the ideas of what could move forward.

Using the streamlined list, we created a map of the study areas, with the areas on the list highlighted. It helped to guide the conversation during the first public meeting because we showed the community members that we had heard them, and it gave them an opportunity to share more ideas. An important note: we framed the activity as "Tell us your ideas" to help people move from identifying the problem to helping us understand some of their ideas.

After the meeting, we added all the public comments to a sheet in our master spreadsheet. We then had one of our junior planners go through all the sheets within the master spreadsheet to condense everything into one new sheet. This included removing duplicates, anything out of scope, and any new maintenance items.

Throughout the project, we documented everything in the master spreadsheet. If something was removed from consideration, we documented why it was removed. If something was added, we documented where we got the recommendation. In the end, we had a final list of recommendations and a timeline for implementation. Figure 5-1 shows how we moved through the process from data collection to final recommendations.

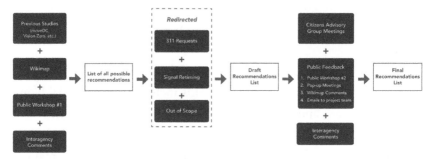

Figure 5-1: Process graphic for a livability study showing a combination of the planning and public engagement processes. (District Department of Transportation)

Opportunity for Reflection

Inclusive transportation starts with including the public in the process. Table 5-1 provides several examples of how I have ensured the public process will inform the planning and design process. The framework is a high-level summary of ways to marry the public engagement process with the planning and design process.

Table 5-1: Public Involvement Framework

Before you begin	• Previous technical analysis • Previous public comments • 311 requests • Social media • Interviews with staff, elected officials, other agencies • Outreach to key stakeholders	Understand the concerns of the community, any promises made to them, and any ideas they have previously shared.

Table 5-1, continued

First meeting	"What did we miss?" "What are your ideas to address the concern?"	Acknowledge previous work and allow the public to add new information.
		Get the public to start providing ideas and alternatives for you to explore.
		Be transparent about constraints and the decision-making process.
		Provide an orientation to the process.
Meeting— alternatives	"What did we miss?" "What do you see as the pros and cons of this alternative?"	Summarize and explain how you used the community's feedback.
		Explain all the alternatives you evaluated and the criteria you used to evaluate.
		Allow public feedback to direct any further analysis.
Meeting—final alternative	"What are some additional considerations as this project moves to design?" "What would enhance this alternative?" "What concerns you about the alternative?"	Summarize and explain how you used the community's feedback. Walk the community through the process and how you determined the final alternative. Share information obtained from the community with the design team as the project moves forward; it should help shape some of the design decisions.
Design phase	Is there something the community is passionate about for which you can have them form a committee during the design process? For example, a committee that selects trees or provides guidance on the color of the rocks or bricks on a retaining wall? Local artists who can lead a community painting?	Keep the community involved as part of the process; community input should involve elements of the design that do not impact safety or have a large impact on cost.

CHAPTER 6

The Task Ahead: Where the Hard Work Continues

WHEN I WAS IN HIGH SCHOOL, I ran track. I was a sprinter, but every now and then I could be convinced to run the 800-meter. The thing about the 800-meter is you could have a quick pace through most of the race, but when you got to that last 200 meters, your legs were tired, your lungs were burning, and everything hurt. But you had to dig deep, give it all you have, and run through the finish line. This chapter is like the last 200 meters of an 800-meter race. You have had a lot thrown at you. We reflected on our personal transportation stories, examined how to define equity, critiqued the transportation industry, analyzed stakeholders, and married the planning and public engagement processes.

Now we must dig deep to make systemic changes to the industry.

Some of the changes I propose in this chapter are low-hanging fruit but still will take at least three to four years to show a noticeable change—if we start now. For some of the changes, we must be ready for the long haul. It could take a generation. Everything in this book rests on six fundamental changes that need to happen in the transportation industry:

1. Moving quicker
2. Directing a vision
3. Enabling bold leadership
4. Increasing diversity
5. Practicing empathy
6. Understanding the opposition

1. Moving Quicker

Traditionally, transportation projects take a long time to go from plan to implementation. Federal regulations require Metropolitan Statistical Areas to have a long-range transportation plan, typically twenty to thirty years into the future. How the plan is developed varies from region to region. Some regions just issue a call for projects, so their plans are a mash-up of ideas from the local jurisdictions. Basically, everyone submits their project and the Metropolitan Planning Organization puts them all in one document without questioning whether that is how the region should invest transportation dollars. Some have a long-range planning process that includes public engagement. Ultimately, the plans are always at least a twenty-year vision, which also includes planning for new people via population and employment changes.

Within that overarching twenty-year-plus plan, state and local governments spend millions of dollars developing plans that will eventually go through the design and construction processes. The challenge for all involved is the timeline. In chapter 1, I mentioned the Intercounty Connector in Maryland, which was originally envisioned in the 1950s. Over the decades, the state would propose the project, then cancel it, and then propose it again. In 1999, I reviewed this project's draft environmental impact statement for a course I was taking. In 2006, I was part of the federal review team for the record of decision. Construction started in 2007 and was completed in 2011. Even with the best-laid plans, major projects can take decades. This means any one person is unlikely to see large transportation projects through from start to finish.

Even at a smaller scale, a roadway reconstruction project in an urban area can take five to ten years from the initial study to completed construction. Planners work with the community on a plan for their neighborhood and everyone gets excited about the recommendations, only to learn they may have to wait five to ten years before construction starts. Then they have to wait another two years until construction is completed.

When it comes to safety and equity, we cannot get so focused on the future people who will live in a community when people who exist today are being injured and inconvenienced by the current transportation system. There is an urgency from the community for us to move faster and show improvements.

Continuing the example of an emergency room from chapter 2, when you break a bone, you go to the ER. The medical team will assess you, maybe take a few X-rays, and then get you stable enough to go home. They will give you orders to follow up with a doctor for a long-term plan, and you will work with that doctor to create a vision for your rehab. For some people, it may be to walk again, but for an elite athlete, the vision may be to break a personal record. Whatever the vision, the doctor develops a plan of action. Similarly, we have communities that need triage today because people are being harmed by the transportation system. The transportation sector needs to put more emphasis on working with communities on short-term solutions that help them stabilize while we also work with them to develop a longer-term solution.

These short-term solutions generally should be low cost to implement. For example, there could be an intersection that needs a narrower geometry so it is safer for people to cross the street. In lieu of a full design process, perhaps delineators could be installed to simulate the curb bulb-outs and narrower crossing. It is low cost and gives everyone the opportunity to see how the intersection performs before the bigger construction investment.

But as easy as this sounds, it can take time to implement. Doing quicker solutions requires resources, both staff and money. With most local governments, it is hard to find any additional resources. Planners and engineers have projects they are currently working to advance. Local governments already have contracts in place with defined scopes. In-house crews have metrics they need to meet. So who is going to design, implement, and monitor the quicker fixes?

It might not be as hard as it sounds! Through natural staff attrition, leaders can restructure positions for a quick-fix team. When it is time to renew contracts, scopes can include additional assistance. It can take two years to have a truly functional quick-fix program for items such as temporary bulb-outs and chicanes—but in the scheme of transportation projects, that is not bad—and it is an important systemic change that can create a lot of good, and goodwill.

However, even quicker fixes may already be within the metrics of the local government that show the community more is coming, such as repairing a broken sidewalk or working with local artists to paint transportation infrastructure such as traffic control boxes or bridge underpasses.

Reflection

What problem can you address immediately so that the community can work with you to develop a long-term vision? Some examples:

- Clean the street with a street sweeper.
- Reinstall a sign.
- Repair a broken sidewalk.
- Install a temporary solution using delineators and pavement markings.

• Repair a pothole.
• Install art on transportation infrastructure.
• Add neighborhood banners to light poles.

2. Directing a Vision

The basis of the long-range transportation plan is population and employment. There is a base year, which is usually the existing condition. In the base year, population and employment are noted around the region as well as the vehicle miles traveled (VMT) for the major roadway facilities. To make the twenty- to thirty-year projection, planners look at potential land use changes over time to project future changes in population and employment. Depending on the region, the projected demographic data are blended with other inputs, such as future mode splits and technology changes, to project future VMT.

While it is great to plan and look toward the future, there are a few challenges with the methodology. One, the modeling does not always capture changes in transportation trends. For example, younger generations are choosing not to get their driver's licenses. According to the Federal Highway Administration, in 2018 the percentage of eighteen-year-olds with a driver's license was 61 percent, down from 80 percent in 1983.[1] Two, the regional forecast models tend to overestimate future demand,[2] meaning resources tend to be overallocated to transportation for cars.

Finally, commute trips by biking, walking, and newer transportation modes such as electric scooters are undercounted. Most cities and regions rely on census and National Household Travel Survey data to determine mode splits. Few examples exist in the United States where there are intentional volume counts for people biking, walking, and using other small modes. At the project level, there may be counts for the specific project area, which can be extrapolated up into a regional model. But all of this falls short of accurately reflecting trips that are not car based.

So how do we do it differently?

One, instead of projecting VMT forward from the existing condition using transportation models, create a model that we can reverse model. For example, what if a region had a bold vision to remove 50 percent of the roadway lane miles within its long-range vision? By setting that as a constraint with the assumed population and employment growth, the model would lay out the transportation options to accomplish that goal. The goal would be a significant investment in modes that can move many people in a small amount of space, such as public transportation, passenger or commuter rail, and bicycle infrastructure.

From a job creation standpoint, it would create plenty of construction jobs to reconstruct roadways into a smaller footprint, including opportunities for new businesses to construct sidewalks and bicycle lanes. It would create jobs for people to operate and maintain vehicles. In addition, it would create jobs to maintain new green spaces that could be created by removing roadways.

Another example on the land use side would be to have a bold vision to remove all surface parking. Rarely is a surface lot the highest and best use of land. Having a vision to remove all surface lots could create space for housing, commercial development, office space, and open space. Parking could be accommodated by parking garages, but hopefully with our bold vision to remove 50 percent of the roadway, there would be less need for parking overall.

Although 50 percent is an arbitrary number and I do not mean it literally, the bigger point is: none of us know what is going to happen in the future. Rather than project from what we can see today, we should be projecting from a vision of what we want life to be in the future. Projections based on the past are why we end up with wide roads.

Similarly with technology: setting a vision and a framework provides tech companies with guidelines for how to operate in your community. The ultimate goals of the technology company are proof of concept and return on investment, which can come at the expense of certain communities. By having a clear vision, you can set the ground rules. You can create an inclusive process to set policies and metrics as new technologies come to the market.

Reflection

How big is your vision? How big is the vision of the community? Are you limited by what you think is possible? For consideration:

- Create tables with community members to understand their vision of the future. Do they see themselves getting on a high-speed train to travel across the country? Do they see themselves living like the Jetsons?
- What must happen to bring that vision to fruition? To use the "reduce all surface parking lots" example, you may need to develop a new land use plan, ultimately changing the parking minimums and maximums, developing a public transit route, creating ways to get there by walking and biking, and so forth.
- What is the framework or what are the strategies for achieving the vision?
- What is the one small thing you can start doing to get you there?

3. Enabling Bold Leadership

As stated throughout the book, elevating new approaches to transportation planning and design will require bold leadership. One challenge is that many decision-makers in transportation are either elected or appointed. Elected officials want to get reelected. Those holding appointed positions serve at the pleasure of the elected leaders. There is a need to navigate politics, but bold leadership is willing to take risk, particularly now, when there is an urgent need to reclaim roadway space for multiple modes.

For example, former New York City transportation commissioner Janette Sadik-Khan was able to close street lanes around Times Square because of support from former mayor Michael Bloomberg. Times Square, despite being the place where thousands brave the elements to watch the ball drop to welcome each new year, was hostile to people not in vehicles. Sadik-Khan notes in her book *Streetfight* that every day, more than 350,000 people walked through Times Square. However, regarding the allocation of space, people had about 10 percent of the public space, and 90 percent was given to cars. Under her leadership, the New York City Department of Transportation temporarily, then permanently, closed streets around Times Square to cars.[3] She was met with resistance, but thanks to her bold thinking and the support of the mayor, they created one the most activated plazas in the United States. Having been in Times Square post-implementation, I believe that New York City actually needs more room for people to move around the area. Fortunately, the success of that project allowed other projects in the city to move forward, such as bus-only lanes.

Leaders of transportation agencies need to know that the elected leadership is committed to a shift in thinking and implementation. Elected leadership needs to know that the leaders of the transportation agencies are working with communities to make the best decisions. There has to be both.

Let's be honest. A bold leader of a transportation agency risks being ousted if the elected leader is more concerned about being reelected or pleasing a particular group of people than they are committed to the bigger vision. A bold elected leader risks failed campaign promises if the leader of the transportation agency is not willing to keep moving forward even when the project generates vocal opposition.

If you have a vision of transportation options, bold leadership means electing, holding accountable, and supporting leaders who embody that vision. Bold leadership may present itself differently depending on the local culture of the community. If you support bold projects, you need to make sure to show it.

Reflection

What will you do to ensure that the right leaders are in place in your community? Some ideas:

- Hold candidate forums in which you ask questions specific to transportation, equity, and inclusive communities.
- Develop candidate questionnaires specific to transportation, equity, and inclusive communities and share them on a website.
- For groups that have an advocacy focus, consider endorsing candidates via press releases, a public website, social media, targeted email lists, or all of these.
- Conduct email and social media campaigns to thank elected leaders and government staff when they make hard decisions.
- When elected leaders are building their government leadership teams, recommend people by name, including their résumés and why you support them. Bonus if you can get on the transition team to have more direct involvement.

Note: for nonprofit groups that have 501(c)(3) status, please consult the Internal Revenue Service for the rules regarding political endorsements, lobbying, and advocacy.

4. Increasing Diversity

Part of the reason why in chapter 1 I had you evaluate your lived experiences as they relate to transportation is that those shape who you are as a professional, consciously and unconsciously.

The beauty of the diversity of a project team is people being able to bring their professional and lived experiences to the table. The reality is that no matter how many years of professional experience we have, we are limited by our lived experiences. For example, other than needing to wear glasses, I do not have any disabilities. Although there are design guides that help to ensure compliance with the Americans with Disabilities Act of 1990, I do not have the lived experience of navigating the world without being able to see, to hear, or to move without the need of assistance, or without needing to avoid overstimulation.

Although the transportation industry today looks different from that of the 1960s, it is still largely White- and male-dominated. It is hard to tease out the specifics, but if you look at the two main professions within transportation—urban planning and civil engineering—more than 50 percent of the planners in the United States are men, and more than 75 percent are White.[4] Within civil engineering, 83.4 percent are men and 71.3 percent are White (non-Hispanic).[5] I have not been able to find good statistics on people with disabilities within the profession. Needless to say, we have more work to do.

In the short term, we have to be more intentional in staff recruitment, particularly for leadership roles. This may require hiring headhunters. Often, it will mean building relationships with colleges and universities that have planning and engineering programs. Both current students and alumni are potential candidates.

In tandem with recruitment, we have to ensure the environment is inclusive in order to retain staff. It does no good to have a diverse workforce if the environment is hostile because someone speaks English with an accent or women are constantly being talked over in meetings.

For small businesses that can participate in transportation projects, we need to reduce the barriers to entry. The US Department of Transportation has a Disadvantaged Business Enterprise program, which is intended to aid entry to doing business with state or local transportation agencies. As a former business owner, I can tell you the process was daunting; the amount of paperwork and documentation to prove I was disadvantaged was almost a ream of paper. Even with the online system, it is a burdensome process. Despite it being a universal form, some state departments of transportation require you to submit all the same documentation to them. For small business owners, the option is either to pay thousands of dollars to a consultant to help you with the paperwork or to take time away from making money to do it yourself. My company eventually had to hire an administrative assistant, who spent half of her time managing the disadvantaged business certifications.

A quick fix would be to have a universal certification that allows for information to be shared between states. That would allow small businesses to focus on projects to make money and create local jobs.

Over the long term, we have to do more to demystify and diversify the profession to increase the number of women, people of color, persons with disabilities, veterans, people with diverse sexual and gender identities, and others so we may reflect the communities we serve. Some of this starts with early childhood education to get children of diverse backgrounds excited about science, technology, engineering, and math. We must teach young people about planning—it is powerful to understand why your community looks the way it does, whether you grow up to be a professional planner or not.

Although no one pointed out to me what I was doing, as a child I started my planning education in my basement. I had an entire Little

People community—a house, a day-care center, an airport, a parking garage, and a farm. I laid everything out on the floor with my Lionel train set, which looped around the community. In my mind, I was just playing and using my imagination. But to my parents, I was planning and managing a community.

What is most exciting about the potential future of transportation is that it is nothing we have seen or experienced before. I am excited about the next few generations. Many have been born into an inclusive society and technology. They are not limited by the baggage of history and Naysayers' ideas of what is and is not possible.

Yes, that takes a generation. But so do transportation projects.

Reflection

In the short and long terms, what specific actions will you take to increase the diversity of the profession? Some examples:

- Share job postings with great candidates and encourage them to apply.
- Be a champion for opportunities for people such as by submitting names for potential candidates or small business partners.
- Volunteer with children to get them interested in the profession— talk to a class, participate in an after-school program, judge a science contest.
- Amplify diverse voices on social media.

5. Practicing Empathy

But diversity is not an out.

One of my favorite television series is *The Good Place*. Its premise, no spoilers, is the philosophical questioning of morality and ethics. Throughout the series, the main characters explore some elements of

T. M. Scanlon's book *What We Owe to Each Other*, tackling topics such as social contracts and our duties to each other as humans. Full disclosure: I have not read the book, but the title grabbed my attention, and the ideas are relevant to our work in transportation.

Social contracts are what we agree to—a set of rules we all agree to live by together.

As discussed in the previous chapters, it seems the same people are repeatedly harmed by decisions made by planners, engineers, and politicians involved in the transportation system. Even the most robust public engagement processes can lead to poor results. To prevent the mistakes of the past, we have an opportunity to create a new framework based on the principles of justice.

According to the *Oxford English Dictionary*, empathy is "the ability to understand and share the feelings of another."

The basis of the civil engineering profession is civilization. The planning profession is about planning a future for people: where they live, work, play, worship, enjoy nature—and how they get to the places where they can do all those things. The professions exist *for people*. To be able to plan and engineer for people, you have to have an understanding of people beyond your own lived experiences.

This means you must really put in the effort to center someone else's lived experience. When was the last time you observed or listened—without judgment—to someone else's life experience? Do not miss the "without judgment" part of that question. It means that as someone shares their experience you do not counter with the latest research or a statement like "Not all [men, White people, heterosexual people, cisgender people, or people without disabilities] . . ." It also means you may hear some things that make you uncomfortable. Lean into that discomfort. It is okay. Why are you feeling uncomfortable? If you feel the need to counter what they are saying, why?

In practical terms, step out of your comfort zone and attend a conference, conversation, panel, or similar event at which the panelists or presenters look nothing like you. For example, attend a conference for people with disabilities to observe, listen, and learn about the challenges they face as they move and exist in the world beyond the missing curb ramp or sidewalk. Follow the voices on social media of people who are Black, Latino or Hispanic, or Indigenous people, other people of color, people with disabilities, or members of the LGBTQ community.

A few years ago, I attended a Complete Streets Coalition dinner, and tamika l. butler was a keynote speaker. At the beginning of her talk, she asked the attendees, who happened to be majority White, if they had heard of a documentary that was highly popular at the time and being discussed among Black people on social media, in barbershops, and in salons. All of the Black people and people of color and two or three White people raised their hand. The point tamika was making is that Black people and people of color have to move in a White-dominated culture every day. We have to know what is going on in the lives of White people. However, White people are largely oblivious to the conversations that Black people and other people of color are having.

When the dominant culture is centered on you, it becomes easy to assume that someone else's experience is the same as yours. If you are a White man, it becomes easy not to notice that the entire leadership of your company is mostly White men. If you are able-bodied, it becomes easy to say "Remove a bus stop to speed up the buses; walking two extra blocks is not a big deal."

Building empathy does not have to be a daunting task. You can absolutely dive right into history books and other nonfiction to learn more. It can be as easy as watching a television show in which the majority of the cast is of a different ethnicity. While being a Black woman in the United States brings the intersectionality of bridging worlds, I still make an effort to learn and understand the "others."

I take a few fairly straightforward actions to observe, listen to, and learn from people who have different views of the world. I follow people who have disabilities, Indigenous populations, LGBTQ people, and the intersectionality of multiple identities on social media. This gives me access to their thoughts and ideas. I learn about new authors and researchers who dive into topics that unpack some of their challenges and threats to their existence. I have also started reading fiction books by authors from these communities, where often the protagonist is someone with that identity. You may think this is unrelated to my work, but it all comes back to planning and transportation being about improving people's lives—and even fiction can be a window into how to do this.

Reflection

Building empathy starts with being curious about other people's lived experiences. Some actions:

- On social media, follow different people and different topics, often already curated. For example, I make it a point not just to follow different topics on social media but also to actively observe when there are social media questions and answers or people are discussing a current event within that community.
- Read nonfiction and fiction books that center on people who are different from you.
- Watch documentaries and shows that center on nondominant cultures.
- Expand your social circles.
- Attend conferences that center on different people. For example, attend a conference that centers on people with disabilities. Observe everything from how the conference is laid out to help people navigate between sessions to the challenges and opportunities of that community.

• Attend cultural heritage tours in communities you work in to learn
more about the history.

As you stretch your empathy muscle, it is okay to not have an opinion, and you will probably make mistakes. Actively observing and learning is completely acceptable.

6. Understanding the Opposition

If everyone believed multimodal transportation was the best approach,
it would be much easier to make progress. But that is not our current
reality—and it may never be, in the United States. However, there is
no war on cars, and not in a modified *Fight Club* movie way: "The first
rule of [the war on cars] is there is no [war on cars]." Today, there are
communities that depend on public transit, walking, and biking to get
to work, school, and errands. They are often the Silently Suffering—
because between a car loan, gas, insurance, and maintenance, owning a
car is expensive. That is at an individual level. In the bigger picture, as
our population continues to grow, expecting people to drive will only
increase traffic congestion.

We are not at war, but we may have philosophical disagreements. It
is important to know the systemic Naysayers. The people who are perfectly fine with destroying communities and the environment so they
can travel faster on the highway. The people who are perfectly fine with
unsafe streets as long as they do not have to slow down or maybe wait
an extra cycle at a traffic light.

Reconciling this opposition is the hardest of all because you must be
committed to change for the long haul. You cannot organize one project
and then pat yourself on the back for a job well done.

It is important that we have this conversation. The forces against
using transportation to reconnect communities are organized, they are

focused, and they have a way of taking messages and distorting them for their own use. As I mentioned before, nationally, any mention of equity gets labeled "critical race theory." People who may not be opposed to hiring their deaf neighbor as a traffic engineer may vehemently oppose critical race theory. It can be difficult to cut through the sound bites and appeal to humanity.

I like to quote these rap lyrics from Yasiin Bay, formerly known as Mos Def, to describe the system we are pushing against:

They say they want you successful
Then they make it stressful
You start keeping pace
They start changing up the tempo

It goes back to a question I asked in the preface. How do you change a system that does not want to change? How do you find common ground with people who are frightened that change would inconvenience them, who deny the injustices their lifestyles inflict on neighbors? It is not a task for the faint of heart.

Reflection

It is important to be equally organized and focused. You have to be willing to focus on the short and long terms at the same time. Some actions:

- Propose candidates for all levels of government, including, but not limited to, planning commissions, zoning boards, transportation commissions, civic club presidents, council members, county commissioners, and advisory councils. If getting started feels overwhelming, then start with advisory councils. Some communities have them for bicycles, disabilities, transit, or pedestrians. It is a nice entry into understanding how your specific government works and starts a leadership pipeline for higher offices.

• Conduct marketing campaigns.
• Engage in grassroots advocacy—go door to door to get support.
• Build coalitions with other organizations.

Crossing the Finish Line

We have the monumental task of righting the wrongs of our predecessors while charting the course for the generations that come after us. This is a task that will require courage, boldness, and empathy as we push against forces in the industry that are resistant to change. It is a task that will require less engineering and planning from behind a computer and more engagement and collaboration with communities.

As you advance in your career, whether in the public sector, consulting, or academia, remember one fundamental truth. Our profession exists to serve people. The technical knowledge you gain throughout your career will serve you well. The time you spend getting to know the communities where you have projects will serve the world well.

What do you owe the world? You owe the world your brilliance and your empathy.

Acknowledgments

In July 2020, it was clear. We are doing it. We are writing a book.

The election of 2020 gave us one of the greatest GIFs (which are short videos, usually without sound, if you are reading this at a future time when GIFs no longer exist). The presumptive vice president, Kamala Harris, has her hair in a low bun, and she's wearing sweats and sunglasses. As she holds a cell phone to her ear, words pop up: "We did it. We did it, Joe." That is how I feel as I close out this book with acknowledgments. My name is on the cover, but "We did it."

In all I do in life, I have to give honor and glory to the Creator of the Universe. The one who has ordered my steps. More than I could express in this book, this has been a journey of faith. There were moments when I wanted to give up, when life was just too chaotic for me to have the clarity to write. Prayer was the only way through. Prayers for wisdom and discernment. Prayers for calm energy. Prayers for the words to flow.

Next, I honor and venerate my ancestors, on whose shoulders I stand. My story does not begin in a hospital in Virginia. It begins with my parents, their parents, their parents' parents, and so forth. I think about my parents, born during the Jim Crow era in the American South, who were in their early twenties when the Reverend Dr. Martin Luther King Jr. was assassinated. My maternal grandparents were educators in Louisiana. My paternal grandparents owned multiple businesses. I interviewed my grandmother before her passing, and she talked about owning a grocery store in Georgia before my dad was born. As a former business owner, I know the blood, sweat, and tears (so many tears) it took to build a business in a world that has programs for women and Black business owners. They did it in Georgia. The South. During Jim Crow. My ancestors were enslaved in this country. They built untold wealth for White landowners. From the bows of a ship to me graduating from an Ivy League institution. Now, that is a testimony.

I could not have done this without my husband, Nick Tobenkin. My friend and confidant. The person who "gets" me and who makes me laugh. In our ketubah, which is a marriage contract in the Jewish faith, there is a line, "May our love provide us with the freedom to be ourselves, and the courage to follow our mutual and individual paths." Thank you, Nick, for supporting me on this path and always being who I need in each moment.

During this journey, my child, Eliana, was born. She is one of my "whys" in life. Just as I stand on the shoulders of my ancestors, she stands on my husband's and mine. As of initial publication of this book, she is a toddler. I admire her sense of humor, honesty, and curiosity. I will never forget a moment when she was seven months old and there was a full moon. I was holding her in the rocking chair, and her eyes were fixated on the moon. It was her first time seeing it. I love being able to experience the world with her. That is her gift to me.

Thanks to my big sister, Dr. Esa M. Davis. It has never been easy to live in her shadow. But she never made me feel small. She continues to set the bar high and achieves with dignity and grace. She has always believed in me and has been in my corner. My protector and my first mentor.

Now, they say do not start listing names because you run the risk of forgetting people. In writing the chapters, it was a privilege to be able to lift up the voices and writings of Black scholars, planners, and architects whom I have the honor of calling friends. But there are people who are part of my brain trust and heart trust whom I have to acknowledge.

There is the family you are given and the family that you find. God has blessed me with a crew of people whom I have known for almost all my life. They have been there for all the milestones. Thanks to Chimera Bowen, Marlon Meade, and Nicole Woodland for being a constant source of encouragement.

Chanceé Lundy, my dear friend and cofounder of Nspiregreen. We took a seed of an idea and grew a business. Much of what is written about in this book we did together. Together we experienced heartache, disappointment, and loss. Psalm 30:5 says, "Weeping may endure for a night, but joy cometh in the morning." That joy. I am so glad I got to experience the joy with her. I pray she receives more than her heart desires.

In alphabetical order by last name: Dara Baldwin, R. Keith Benjamin, Charles Brown, tamika l. butler, Anita Cozart, Vedette Gavin, Odetta MacLeish-White, and Ascala Sisk. People for whom I have the highest respect. We have brainstormed and published writings together. Whether with a quick "You good, sis?," a gentle correction, or a real talk conversation, they have been there. Even when down to the final context reviews of this book, they read each page and provided feedback and recommended edits.

There are many others who have been part of my journey. I thank all of them.

Last and most certainly not least, thanks to my editor, Courtney Lix. In October 2018, she walked up to me at the end of a session at a conference and said, "Have you ever thought about writing a book?"

Over the course of months, I decided that I was writing a book. I started writing, and then I wanted to stop writing. Courtney was there encouraging, urging, and prompting me to write. So we are here. We did it!

Notes

Introduction

1. The social determinants of health (SDOH) constitute a framework for the elements that impact people's well-being, health, and quality of life. Centers for Disease Control and Prevention, "Social Determinants of Health: Know What Affects Health," accessed December 4, 2021, https://www.cdc.gov/socialdeterminants/index.htm.

2. Pivotal Ventures and McKinsey & Company, "Rebooting Representation: Using CSR and Philanthropy to Close the Gender Gap in Tech," accessed December 4, 2021, https://www.rebootrepresentation.org/wp-content/uploads/Rebooting-Representation-Report.pdf.

3. Benjamin Wilson, Judy Hoffman, and Jamie Morgenstern, "Predictive Inequity in Object Detection," Cornell University ArXiv, Computer Science, arXiv:1902.11097, February 21, 2019, https://arxiv.org/pdf/1902.11097.pdf, https://doi.org/10.48550/arXiv.1902.11097.

4. Anita Hamilton, "How Bike Share Systems Are Failing Us," Vice, August 21, 2018, https://www.vice.com/en/article/ne5yeg/bike-share-systems-fail-underserved-communities.

5. Matthew Burke et al., "Study: City Visitors Who Use E-Scooters More Spend More," Streetsblog USA, June 29, 2021, https://usa.streetsblog.org/2021/06/29/study-city-visitors-who-use-e-scooters-more-spend-more/.

6. Josh Cohen, "Seattle Test Will Lead to Regulating Dockless Bike-Share,"

Next City, December 21, 2017, https://nextcity.org/daily/entry/seattle
-dockless-bikeshare-pilot-regulation.

7. The statement about pedestrian fatalities was based on the 2021 edition of
"Dangerous by Design." After the final edits of this book were completed,
the 2022 edition of "Dangerous by Design" was released. Smart Growth
America, "Dangerous by Design 2022," accessed December 4, 2021,
https://smartgrowthamerica.org/dangerous-by-design/.

8. Raj Chetty and Nathaniel Hendren, "The Impacts of Neighborhoods on
Intergenerational Mobility," Harvard University, April 2015, http://www
.equality-of-opportunity.org/images/nbhds_exec_summary.pdf.

9. Veronica O. Davis, "Why Is Capital Bikeshare Usage Low East of the
River?," *Greater Greater Washington* (blog), January 31, 2011, https://
ggwash.org/view/8097/why-is-capital-bikeshare-usage-low-east-of-the
-river.

10. Better Bike Share Partnership, "Who We Are," accessed September 10,
2022, https://betterbikeshare.org/about/who-we-are/.

11. L. Dara Baldwin et al., "My Back Is Still the Bridge," in "The White
Problem in Planning," ed. William Curran-Groome, special issue, *Carolina Planning Journal* 46 (2021): 79–90, https://issuu.com/carolina
planningjournal/docs/vol_46_whiteproblem_in_planning.

12. National Highway Traffic Safety Administration, "2020 Fatality Data
Show Increased Traffic Fatalities during Pandemic," June 3, 2021, https://
www.nhtsa.gov/press-releases/2020-fatality-data-show-increased-traffic
-fatalities-during-pandemic.

13. National Highway Traffic Safety Administration, "USDOT Releases
New Data Showing That Road Fatalities Spiked in First Half of 2021,"
October 28, 2021, https://www.nhtsa.gov/press-releases/usdot-releases
-new-data-showing-road-fatalities-spiked-first-half-2021.

14. Chicago Council on Global Affairs, "Reclaiming the Right to the City,"
September 2021, https://www.thechicagocouncil.org/sites/default/files
/2021-09/CCGA%20Reclaiming%20the%20Right%20to%20the%20
City_vFb.pdf.

15. Destiny Thomas, "'Safe Streets' Are Not Safe for Black Lives," Bloomberg
CityLab, June 8, 2020, https://www.bloomberg.com/news/articles/2020
-06-08/-safe-streets-are-not-safe-for-black-lives.

Chapter 1: Transportation Is Personal

1. Not much documentation exists about the impact of the I-10 highway. This article confirms my mom's memory of the high school being torn down for I-10. She graduated from St. Francis Xavier High School in 1961. Bonny Van, "Century of Educational Excellence," *Catholic Commentator*, accessed February 15, 2022, http://thecatholiccommentator .org/pages/?p=52187.

2. Farrell Evans, "How Interstate Highways Gutted Communities—and Reinforced Segregation," *History*, October 20, 2021, https://www.history .com/news/interstate-highway-system-infrastructure-construction -segregation.

3. United Nations Academic Impact, "Capacity-Building," https://www .un.org/en/academic-impact/capacity-building.

4. Courtland Milloy, "D.C. Election Didn't Just Unseat Abrasive Mayor Fenty. It Was a Populist Revolt," *Washington Post*, September 16, 2010, https://www.washingtonpost.com/wp-dyn/content/article/2010/09/15 /AR2010091506240.html.

5. Courtland Milloy, "Bicyclist Bullies Try to Rule the Road in D.C.," *Washington Post*, July 8, 2014, https://www.washingtonpost.com/local /bicyclist-bullies-try-to-rule-the-road-in-dc/2014/07/08/f7843560-06e3 -11e4-bbf1-cc51275e7f8f_story.html?hpid=z3.

6. Courtland Milloy, "A Spin with the D.C. Bicycle Crowd Leads to a Tad More Sympathy," *Washington Post*, August 10, 2014, https://www.wash ingtonpost.com/local/a-spin-with-the-dc-bicycle-crowd-leads-to-a-tad -more-sympathy/2014/08/10/1a271c08-20b2-11e4-8593-da634b334390 _story.html.

7. National Society of Black Engineers, "About Us," https://www.nsbe.org /about-us.

8. Kate Rushin, "The Bridge Poem," in *This Bridge Called My Back: Writings by Radical Women of Color*, 2nd ed., ed. Cherríe Moraga and Gloria Anzaldúa (New York: Kitchen Table: Women of Color Press, 1983).

9. L. Dara Baldwin et al., "My Back Is Still the Bridge," in "The White Problem in Planning," ed. William Curran-Groome, special issue, *Carolina Planning Journal* 46 (2021): 79–90, https://issuu.com/carolina planningjournal/docs/vol_46_whiteproblem_in_planning.

10. US Census Bureau, "Mode of Transportation to Work: Worked from

Home," 2006–2019 American Community Survey, https://www2.census
.gov/programs-surveys/commuting/guidance/acs-1yr/DY2019-Percent
-worked-from-home.pdf.

11. Patrick Coate, "Remote Work before, during, and after the Pandemic,"
National Council on Compensation Insurance, January 25, 2021, https://
www.ncci.com/SecureDocuments/QEB/QEB_Q4_2020_RemoteWork
.html.

12. Michelle Fox, "The Great Resignation Has Changed the Workplace for
Good," CNBC, May 10, 2022, https://www.cnbc.com/2022/05/10/-the
-great-resignation-has-changed-the-workplace-for-good-.html.

13. Douglass B. Lee Jr., Lisa A. Klein, and Gregorio Camus, "Induced Traffic
and Induced Demand," *Journal of the Transportation Research Board* 1659,
no. 1 (1999): 68–75, https://doi.org/10.3141/1659-09.

Chapter 2: Equity Is More than a Baseball Graphic

1. Todd Litman, "Evaluating Transportation Equity: Guidance for Incorpo-
rating Distributional Impacts in Transportation Planning," Victoria Transport Policy Institute, June 11, 2014, https://nacto.org/wp-content
/uploads/2015/07/2014_Litman_Evaluating-Transportation-Equity.pdf.

2. Anne Hudson, "Making Equity Real: A Conversation with tamika l.
butler, Esq.," MIT Mobility Initiative, November 19, 2020, https://www
.colab.mit.edu/colabradio-more/tamika-butler.

3. *Merriam-Webster.com Dictionary*, s.v. "equity," accessed September 19,
2022, https://www.merriam-webster.com/dictionary/equity.

4. New York State Transportation Equity Alliance, "About Us," accessed
September 19, 2022, http://nystea.net/about-us/.

5. Litman, "Evaluating Transportation Equity."

6. Setha Low, "Public Space and Diversity: Distributive, Procedural, and
Interactional Justice for Parks," in *The Ashgate Research Companion to
Planning and Culture*, ed. Greg Young and Deborah Stevenson (Abing-
don: Routledge, January 2013).

7. Montgomery County Department of Transportation, "Montgomery
County Vision Zero Equity Framework," December 2019, https://www
.montgomerycountymd.gov/visionzero/Resources/Files/Equity%20Task
%20Force%20Framework%20FINAL.pdf, 8.

8. PolicyLink, "The Equity Manifesto," 2018, https://www.policylink.org /sites/default/files/pl_sum15_manifesto_FINAL_2018.pdf.

9. People for Mobility Justice, "Mission," accessed September 19, 2022, https://www.peopleformobilityjustice.org/mission.

Chapter 3: Should There Be a War on Cars?

1. Centers for Disease Control and Prevention, "Transportation Safety," accessed September 19, 2022, https://www.cdc.gov/transportationsafety /index.html.

2. National Safety Council, "Societal Costs," accessed September 19, 2022, https://injuryfacts.nsc.org/all-injuries/costs/societal-costs/.

3. US Environmental Protection Agency, "Carbon Pollution from Transportation," accessed September 19, 2022, https://www.epa.gov/transportation -air-pollution-and-climate-change/carbon-pollution-transportation.

4. American Society of Civil Engineers, "Roads," in "2021 Report Card for America's Infrastructure," https://infrastructurereportcard.org/cat-item /roads/.

5. Elijah Chiland, "Map Shows LA's Red Car System in Its 1920s Heyday," Curbed Los Angeles, September 6, 2018, https://la.curbed.com/2018/9 /6/17825186/los-angeles-streetcar-map-red-pacific-electric.

6. Junxiang Wei et al., "Neighborhood Sidewalk Access and Childhood Obesity," *Obesity Reviews* 22, no. S1 (2021): e13057, https://doi.org/10 .1111/obr.13057.

7. US Department of Health and Human Services, Office of Disease Prevention and Health Promotion, "Social Determinants of Health," accessed December 4, 2021, https://health.gov/healthypeople/objectives-and-data /social-determinants-health.

8. National Academies of Sciences, Engineering, and Medicine, *Highway Capacity Manual, 7th Edition: A Guide for Multimodal Mobility Analysis* (Washington, DC: National Academies Press, 2022).

9. Angie Schmitt, "The Spectacular Waste of Half-Empty Black Friday Parking Lots," Streetsblog USA, December 1, 2014, https://usa.streetsblog .org/2014/12/01/the-spectacular-waste-of-half-empty-black-friday-park ing-lots/.

10. Virginia Department of Transportation, "More on Slugging," last

modified November 1, 2019, https://www.virginiadot.org/travel/how
-virginians-slug-more.asp.

11. Federal Highway Administration, "I-10 LA 415 to Essen Lane on I-10
and I-12 Stage 1 Environmental Assessment Finding of No Significant
Impact and Section 4(f) Evaluation," November 2020, https://i10br.com
/wp-content/uploads/2021/02/H004100_FONSI.pdf.

12. William Taylor Potter, "Report: Louisiana's Roads Cost Drivers $7.6 Bil-
lion a Year," *Lafayette (LA) Daily Advertiser*, April 14, 2021, https://www
.theadvertiser.com/story/news/2021/04/14/report-louisianas-roads-cost
-drivers-7-6-billion-year/7218858002/.

13. Noel King, "A Brief History of How Racism Shaped Interstate Highways,"
NPR, April 7, 2021, https://www.npr.org/2021/04/07/984784455/a
-brief-history-of-how-racism-shaped-interstate-highways.

14. Richard Rothstein, *The Color of Law: A Forgotten History of How Our
Government Segregated America* (New York: Liveright, 2017).

15. Cheryl W. Thompson et al., "Racial Covenants, a Relic of the Past, Are
Still on the Books across the Country," Houston Public Media, November
17, 2021, https://www.houstonpublicmedia.org/npr/2021/11/18
/1049052531/racial-covenants-a-relic-of-the-past-are-still-on-the-books
-across-the-country/.

16. Smart Growth America, "Dangerous by Design 2022," accessed December 4, 2021, https://smartgrowthamerica.org/dangerous-by-design/.

17. Asthma and Allergy Foundation of America, "Asthma Disparities in
America," accessed September 19, 2022, https://www.aafa.org/asthma
-disparities-burden-on-minorities.aspx.

18. Safe Routes to School National Partnership, "Fighting for Equitable
Transportation: Why It Matters," 2015, https://www.apha.org/~/media
/files/pdf/topics/environment/built_environment/srtsnp_equitytransp
_factsheet2015.ashx.

19. Charles T. Brown, "Jaywalking," *Arrested Mobility*, podcast, February
2022, https://arrestedmobility.com/episodes/.

20. American Public Transportation Association, "Public Transit's Safety
Benefits," accessed September 19, 2022, https://www.apta.com/research
-technical-resources/research-reports/public-transit-is-key-strategy-in
-advancing-vision-zero/.

21. American Public Transportation Association, "Who Rides Public

Transportation," January 2017, https://www.apta.com/wp-content/up
loads/Resources/resources/reportsandpublications/Documents/APTA
-Who-Rides-Public-Transportation-2017.pdf.

Chapter 4: Power, Influence, and the Complexity of People

1. Matt Cohen, "DDOT, Church Reach Agreement on M Street Cycletrack.
WABA Isn't Happy," DCist, August 19, 2013, https://dcist.com/story
/13/08/19/heres-why-the-m-street-bike-lane-wo/.

2. Derek S. Hyra, *Race, Class, and Politics in the Cappuccino City* (Chicago:
University of Chicago Press, 2017), 111.

3. Marc Fisher, "O Street Market: Symbol of Violence Becomes a Marker for
D.C.'s Resurgence," *Washington Post*, November 19, 2013, https://www
.washingtonpost.com/local/o-street-market-symbol-of-violence-becomes
-a-marker-for-dcs-resurgence/2013/11/19/52012d2c-4ca9-11e3-9890
-a1e0997fb0c0_story.html.

4. Larry W. Smith, "Stakeholder Analysis: A Pivotal Practice of Successful Projects," paper presented at Project Management Institute Annual
Seminars & Symposium, Houston, TX (Newtown Square, PA: Project
Management Institute, 2000), https://www.pmi.org/learning/library
/stakeholder-analysis-pivotal-practice-projects-8905.

5. Civil Rights Act of 1964, 42 U.S.C. § 2000d.

6. US Department of Transportation, Federal Highway Administration,
"Civil Rights: Toolkit," last modified August 1, 2022, https://www.fhwa
.dot.gov/civilrights/programs/title_vi/toolkit.cfm.

7. In 2018, I had the opportunity to participate in a Salzburg Global
Seminar titled "Building Healthy, Equitable Communities: The Role of
Inclusive Urban Development and Investment." I connected with twelve
other attendees representing three countries to develop "A Call to Action:
Interrogate Power and Analyze Privilege to Create and Sustain Healthy
Communities." What I discuss in this chapter teases out that framework
specifically in relation to transportation.

8. Ascala Sisk and Salzburg Global Fellows, "Confronting Power and Privilege for Inclusive, Equitable and Healthy Communities," April 20, 2020,
https://www.salzburgglobal.org/news/statements/article/confronting
-power-and-privilege-for-inclusive-equitable-and-healthy-communities.

9. Peter D. Kinder, "Not in My Backyard Phenomenon," *Encyclopedia*

Britannica, accessed September 19, 2022, https://www.britannica.com/topic/Not-in-My-Backyard-Phenomenon.

10. Kathy Stewart, "Parking Woes Forcing Churches to Leave D.C.," WTOP News, December 20, 2015, https://wtop.com/local/2015/09/parking-woes-forcing-churches-leave-d-c/.

Chapter 6: The Task Ahead: Where the Hard Work Continues

1. Associated Press, "Kids and Cars: Today's Teens in No Rush to Start Driving," *USA Today*, August 4, 2021, https://www.usatoday.com/story/sports/nascar/2021/08/04/kids-and-cars-todays-teens-in-no-rush-to-start-driving/48148523/.

2. The specific conclusion is "Models that lack feedback tend to overestimate future congestion problems and overestimate capacity expansion benefits." Todd Litman, "Generated Traffic and Induced Travel: Implications for Transport Planning," Victoria Transport Policy Institute, November 2, 2022, https://www.vtpi.org/gentraf.pdf.

3. Janette Sadik-Khan and Seth Solomonow, *Streetfight: Handbook for an Urban Revolution* (New York: Penguin Books, 2017).

4. Data USA, "Urban & Regional Planners," accessed September 19, 2022, https://datausa.io/profile/soc/urban-regional-planners#demographics.

5. Data USA, "Civil Engineers," accessed September 19, 2022, https://datausa.io/profile/soc/civil-engineers#demographics.

About the Author

Veronica O. Davis, PE, is a civil engineer, planner, transportation nerd, public speaker, community activist, guest lecturer, poet, blogger, lover of art, yogi, foodie, world explorer, wife, and mom. When she was twenty-two years old, she wrote a life strategic plan declaring that she would be a world-renowned transportation expert and an author with an eclectic collection of books across multiple genres. The clarity of that vision allows her to achieve her goals.